MASTERS AT WORK

MASTERS AT WORK

BECOMING A VENTURE CAPITALIST

GARY RIVLIN

SIMON & SCHUSTER

New York   London   Toronto   Sydney   New Delhi

Simon & Schuster
1230 Avenue of the Americas
New York, NY 10020

First Simon & Schuster hardcover edition April 2019

SIMON & SCHUSTER and colophon are registered trademarks of
Simon & Schuster, Inc.

For information about special discounts for
bulk purchases, please contact Simon & Schuster Special Sales
at 1-866-506-1949 or business@simonandschuster.com.

The Simon & Schuster Speakers Bureau can bring authors to your live event.
For more information or to book an event, contact the
Simon & Schuster Speakers Bureau at 1-866-248-3049
or visit our website at www.simonspeakers.com.

Manufactured in the United States of America

1   3   5   7   9   10   8   6   4   2

Library of Congress Cataloging-in-Publication Data is available.

ISBN 978-1-5011-6789-8
ISBN 978-1-5011-6790-4 (ebook)

To Oliver and Silas

CONTENTS

BECOMING A
VENTURE CAPITALIST

PROLOGUE

It's been more than twenty years since I first started hanging out with the venture capitalists of Silicon Valley. As it happened, my first encounter was with John Doerr, who is probably the most famous VC who has ever lived. Doerr is not necessarily the best ever, but he might be that as well. Certainly he ranks as the richest, with a net worth of $7.4 billion at the start of 2018.

It was late in 1995, and a newish Silicon Valley magazine (with venture money behind it, naturally) gave me what its editor admitted sounded like a potentially dull assignment: write about what the big cable companies were doing about the internet. I was new to tech, so he started me out with three names. "Talk to this guy Eric Schmidt," he suggested. Schmidt was then the well-respected chief technology officer at Sun Microsystems and not the former CEO of Google with a net worth of nearly $15 billion. I'd end up talking with Schmidt dozens of times over the next decade. The second name on the list was Paul Saffo, a tech prognosticator on the "frequent-call" list of any reporter covering Silicon Valley. He, too, would become a good source. The third name was John Doerr.

Doerr invited me to his office on Sand Hill Road in Menlo Park. There, thirty miles south of San Francisco, in the hills above Stanford University, most of the world's most successful venture capital firms cluster. Most occupy nondescript buildings that could be located in any office park, but his partnership, Kleiner Perkins Caufield & Byers, was royalty in Silicon Valley. Its home then, as today, looked like a ski chalet set among the redwoods. I parked a dusty pickup between late-model BMWs and kicked my feet through puddles of fallen needles to the heavy front doors of Kleiner Perkins, as everyone called the firm, if not simply Kleiner. Inside felt like a Hollywood set: the richest woods, sleek leather couches, exposed beams, expensive artwork on the walls. In the mornings, the staff put out a selection of bagels and spreads with fresh fruit and berries. By the afternoon, the Sub-Zeros were crowded with the leftovers from that day's catered lunch. Most spectacular was the fishbowl conference room in the center of everything. It included an oak conference table so mammoth it had reportedly had to be delivered by helicopter.

Those were still the days of dial-up. Logging on to the internet then meant using a telephone line and mini-modems that squawked and hissed and emitted staticky cries whenever asked to connect to a computer. You cursed when someone sent a large document that took forever to download, and all but the simplest of graphics threatened to crash the old IBM personal computer I was still using. To Saffo and Schmidt, to whom I had spoken already, the cable companies could provide salvation—if they didn't blow it. The wires the cable companies ran into our homes and apartments were much thicker than phone wires and, by comparison, capable of delivering great torrents of data. Saffo, Schmidt, and the other technologists I had talked to all used the same analogy: with cable, it would be as if pumping water through a fire hose rather than through a straw. I didn't know much before I showed up at Kleiner Perkins, but I understood enough to appreciate that the cable companies, big and fat and hated by most of their customers, were sitting on a gold mine.

Doerr wore an open-collared blue oxford and khakis, as did his partners, all of whom were men. (The firm would remain all male until 2010.) It was as if they dressed in uniform. Meanwhile, I felt like an idiot in a sports jacket and tie while the fidgety Doerr, long beaked and bespectacled, birdlike in his movements, quickly ran me through the potential of cable to "absolutely crush it as a commercial mass medium." Cable's thick pipe, Doerr explained, "makes possible the exchange of music and video." It would also allow people to buy and sell things. He mentioned another young start-up he and his partners had recently backed: Amazon.com. Cable, he said, would enable Amazon to build a "fast-moving e-commerce platform," by which he meant a "World Wide Web" (as everyone referred to the web back then, as if required to spell out the *www* at the beginning of virtually all web addresses) robust enough to handle what Amazon's founder, Jeff Bezos, had in mind. "It's going to be more than books," I remember Doerr telling me. I thought at the time he meant they'd also sell music and movies, not everything aside from maybe firearms and livestock.

Venture capitalists besides John Doerr certainly recognized cable's potential to cash in on the internet. I doubt, though, that many matched his conviction or determination. He started attending industry events and reading the industry's niche journals. It was while Doerr was at a trade show in Denver that, over drinks with a few new friends he had made in the cable industry, he sketched out his idea for a company that he had dubbed @Home. This start-up, funded by Kleiner and any cable executive buying into the idea, would allow the cable companies—on paper, at least—to play the unlikely heroes who would save us from chucking our computers out the window while waiting for a single photograph to materialize.

"We're talking about building a new network, from scratch," Doerr said matter-of-factly. "We're really talking about a different model for the internet."

Still, Doerr was confident of success, so much so that he brought up another of his investments: Netscape Communications. Netscape, which had gone public a few months earlier, helped launch the internet age with a free, simple-to-use, downloadable piece of software called Navigator, which allowed users to cruise the web in full technicolor. If anything, Netscape's initial public offering, or IPO (when a private company begins selling shares to the public), would have a greater impact on Silicon Valley over the next few years than even its browser did. A company's market capitalization—more colloquially, its "market cap"—is the total worth of the stock in a company, whether still in the hands of a company's founders or in the portfolios of the giant mutual funds or owned by individual investors. Netscape had a first-day market cap of $2.9 billion—a crazy-high valuation for a sixteen-month-old company that had never made a profit. Netscape would prove the justification for bringing public scores of half-baked companies and the inspiration for countless entrepreneurs seeking to cash in on the internet without the hard work of figuring out how to make money on an idea.

"People say that the internet is being overhyped, but the opposite is true," Doerr told me. "I think it's been underhyped. I think the internet's going to be bigger than television." In a world hungry for bandwidth, he imagined millions of people willing to pay @Home $35 a month for its service, not including installation fees and add-on charges. The company was only around one year old, yet he was already imagining an @Home IPO that would eclipse Netscape's. "I bet we'll have a first-day market cap north of three billion dollars," he proclaimed.

I was new to the tech beat, but even to my neophyte ears, that sounded highly improbable. Adding to its unlikelihood were rival efforts by other companies large and small, including Time Warner's Road Runner service. Even Doerr's name and clout might not be enough to tilt the market in favor of the technologies @Home was selling over those of competitors. The gambler within wanted a piece of that wager. He had a couple of bottles of wine on the credenza behind him, and, on the spot, I proposed a bet: he would buy me a case of a favorite wine of mine if @Home's market cap fell short of $3 billion. I would do the same for him if it had a first-day close above that amount.

Doerr took the bet. And the next day he canceled it, telling me in an email that he didn't like the idea of giving me an incentive to root against @Home's success. That was too bad for me. I would've won a case of wine that I couldn't afford after @Home went public in 1997. Yet I was hardly able to gloat. Although the company was still losing millions of dollars each month at the time of its IPO and could claim only modest revenues, @Home fell only around $100 million short of the $3 billion mark. I was amazed he had come so close: a stock market value of several billion dollars for an idea scrawled on a cocktail napkin only a few years earlier.

1

THE PITCH

Greylock Partners maintains not one but two offices in the San Francisco Bay Area. One is on Sand Hill Road, in Menlo Park, the Wall Street of venture capital and more or less in the middle of Silicon Valley. But these days the center of gravity in the tech world has shifted north to San Francisco, and Greylock, like most of the area's top venture firms, now leases space in the city. Josh Elman, regarded widely as one of venture's bright new stars, is working out of Greylock's San Francisco offices on a sunny Wednesday in the fall of 2017. It's there, in a factory-chic office in a part of town thick with start-ups and rival venture firms, that I join him for a lineup of meetings that includes a sit-down with the founder of a mobile-app start-up that's been around for several years. "This is someone I've known a long time," Elman tells me. "From before I was a VC."

The ground rules of this interview dictate that I can't

name the entrepreneur or his start-up. But there's no stopping me from describing the man as an odd duck. I've sat in on my share of pitch meetings over the years. I've witnessed awkward mumblers who can't make eye contact. In the late 1990s, at the peak of the dot-com madness, I tried not to visibly roll my eyes over the hubris of the MBAs descending on Silicon Valley with their charts and projections but not much else beyond a smooth, practiced delivery and the promise of "ubiquity" for whatever they were selling. But never had I come across an entrepreneur as buttoned-down bland as this one. His background was an interesting one that included a stint on Wall Street. He was older than the typical founder. Yet he didn't seem to have the personality to lead a growing tech start-up.

The CEO claims that he isn't at Greylock looking for money. "We're not in fund-raising mode," he says to me as we're introducing ourselves to each other. As the founder tells it, he's just one old colleague asking another for friendly advice as he preps himself to raise a large slug of money. The CEO takes a seat across a conference table from Elman and plugs in his laptop loaded with a multi-slide presentation that he thinks is worth at least $50 million. To his right sits a top executive from his company: a wiry man with a shaved head, a deep résumé, and an intensity that suggests he would crash through a wall if that's what it would take to win. "We literally were making changes in the car a few minutes ago," the CEO tells Elman. He's aiming for nonchalance, but it comes off as an obvious ploy to lower the stakes on a high-stakes meeting. He has no doubt been sweating this meeting—and every slide—for weeks.

Greylock is one of the country's oldest venture firms and among the most highly regarded. It might be overstating things some to say that pitching Greylock (as a *Newsweek* contributor wrote in 2014) "is a bit like being a rookie pitcher stepping onto the mound at Yankee Stadium—with Babe Ruth walking up to the plate." But there was no doubting the firm's supremacy. I would speak to more than two dozen industry people for this book. Almost to a person, they listed Greylock as a top-five venture firm, if not top three. Greylock had been an early investor in both LinkedIn and Facebook, when $27.5 million bought nearly 6 percent of a company today worth more than $500 billion; and also the music-streaming service Pandora, which was worth $2.6 billion at the end of its first day as a publicly traded stock in 2011. Greylock Partners had also invested in Instagram, the thirteen-person start-up that Facebook bought for $1 billion in 2012; Tumblr, the microblogging company that Yahoo purchased for $1.1 billion in 2013; Zipcar, which Avis paid $500 million for that same year; Dropbox (a digital storage service), valued at $12.7 billion when it went public in 2018; and also Medium (an online publisher) and Airbnb. Greylock had the economic means to provide the CEO with the money he needed to build out his idea and also the connections of Elman and his partners, along with the services of the eight full-time recruiters who work for Greylock and its in-house communications team if a start-up team needs help with its messaging. (A lot of the big firms provide these kinds of ancillary services, to increase the chances that the portfolio companies they fund are winners.) Quite simply, Elman could make his company.

This is not the CEO's first time pitching Elman. That's obvious a minute or two into the meeting. "I want to start by thanking you for calling BS on our numbers the last time we met," the man says. Elman fills me in later. A year or two earlier, the CEO had offered revenue estimates based on the brightest assumptions—"and then basically he doubled everything." But apparently Elman has a soft spot for the CEO. Or at least he sees potential in his company. The CEO had been struggling to find the right business model, and Elman has been helping him find the right market for his app, even if he hasn't been willing to invest yet. Now, several business models later, the CEO is certain the company is positioned where it needs to be. "We really appreciate all you've done to help us hone the business," he says. A small smile appears briefly on his face but disappears immediately, as if someone has snapped shut the blinds.

"I'm just trying to be a blank slate here," Elman says helpfully. The VC is of average height, with the chunky build of someone for whom exercise is largely speed walking between meetings. He has thinning hair and blue eyes behind a pair of stylish metal glasses. On this day, he's dressed in a blue T-shirt under an untucked plaid shirt, jeans, and running shoes. He's an upbeat, if fidgety, presence in the room, with a puppy-dog spirit, all nods and smiles. He almost leans into the presentation, as if primed to be delighted by whatever an entrepreneur might utter next.

Elman wants to fall in love. The CEO, however, is making it hard. An early slide boasts of the tens of millions of venture dollars his company has already raised. The smile dissolves from Elman's face. His fingers absentmindedly find a pen and begin playing with it. The VC within seems almost offended that a founder is boasting of blowing all that money in search of the right market. Elman lets another slide or two pass but then asks the CEO to go back. "You save that for the end," he says of the amount of venture money raised already. Later, he is blunter: "He had burned through"—here he gives the exact number, but, suffice it to say, it was closer to $100 million than to zero. "And he's putting that up at the top of his slide deck like a selling point?"

Every industry has its own vocabulary. The shorthand and jargon can sound like gibberish to an outsider, but they form a code that offers entry into that world. The CEO talks of "legacy systems" hobbled by "the premobile economic model" and "organic" versus "paid" growth, which has allowed them to pick up users without much in the way of customer "acquisition costs." All of it is encouraging news for a mobile-app maker wanting to be on the smartphones of hundreds of millions of people around the globe. Millions have already downloaded the app, and, if most aren't yet paying customers, the CEO shares some clever ideas for getting anxious parents and others to pay monthly for the premium services they're selling.

He flashes a couple of slides showing the market share enjoyed by some of those "legacy" companies (big, established brands that are rarely tech savvy enough to offer much in the way of competition). The numbers are tantalizingly large. The actual revenues they've already generated are similarly impressive: multimillion-dollar payments from third parties seeking access to the audience they are aggregating, with the promise of much more. The smile is back on Elman's face.

"This is the first time in a meeting with you where I get the investment thesis," Elman says. He does some quick math in his head and encourages the founder to be bolder in his pitch. "Play up that this is a 'billion-dollar opportunity,'" he suggests.

Elman is an observant, fast-thinking, fast-talking guy; he doesn't seem to miss much. The CEO is more the opposite and slow to pick up on social cues. Dour and lacking emotion, he plods through a prepared presentation—which Elman continues to interrupt. "Go back a slide," he tells the CEO. The revenue projections are on the screen again. "The big question is defensibility," he says. "Couldn't any number of big companies do exactly what you're doing?" he asks and then lists several, including Google and Facebook. "How do we know you're the only ones who can cash in on this honeypot?" Looking at me, Elman says, "That's always the question."

The CEO doesn't attack the answer so much as brush it aside. But here his sidekick offers a far more convincing argument that gets Elman nodding and smiling happily.

The three of them talk about the company name: Do they need to change it? And, despite how much they've already spent establishing a brand, do they also need to change the company slogan? Elman shifts in his chair and starts fiddling with a paper clip. Another slide gets him talking about burn rate: the money a company spends on salaries and other costs each month. Prior to becoming a venture capitalist, Elman worked at Facebook and Twitter. He knows something about growing a tech company.

Elman points out that the CEO has been burning through less than $1 million a month. "If you ramped up your burn rate to closer to three million, no one would freak out," he advises. From where I'm sitting, the message is unmistakably clear: Elman is telling his old colleague to mash his foot down hard on the gas pedal. But rather than pause to consider the VC's comment, the CEO bats it down, saying dismissively, "I'm like a Depression baby when it comes to spending."

Every venture deal gets reduced to what is called the "valuation"—the paper worth of a company—so that the investors can figure out their ownership stakes. For example, a start-up is valued at $20 million (the "premoney" valuation) if the venture capitalists are spending $5 million to buy a 20 percent share in the company, or one-fifth of $25 million (the "postmoney valuation"). The CEO, perhaps feeling emboldened by Elman's encouragement, offers, "I think it should be a $750 million valuation." One of the legacy companies whose business he's threatening has told him it wants to invest in the next round. But he'll still need to find venture investors if he's going to raise the kind of money he's seeking.

Elman squirms in his seat. He pulls at his face and tugs at his clothes. It's never easy to bring up what venture capitalists call a down round. The tech graveyard is crowded with companies that were valued at $400 million when they raised a C round (a third round of funding) but only $200 million (rather than, say, the $800 million valuation the founders had been counting on) on the D round. That dilutes the ownership rate of a company's founders and initial investors—and also all those early employees who had been hired with the promise of owning a sliver of the company. Elman suggests the possibility of a down round, but the CEO shudders at the distasteful prospect of bursting the bubble of all his hotshot programmers who are banking on a big payoff once the company hits it big.

"My engineers would mutiny if I even bring up a down round," the CEO says, slamming shut the door on further conversation.

The rest of the meeting has Elman offering several more pieces of advice. "It's time to pull together a narrative," he tells the two men, by which he means they need to do a better job of presenting their story. He also suggests that they play up what he calls "engagement data": stats that show how often and for how long customers use their service.

The art of being a venture capitalist means never saying no even if you rarely say yes. Greylock Partners met with several thousand entrepreneurs in 2016—and made sixteen investments that year. Yet what if the start-up that struck you as a dud in a first round—the A round—catches fire, and you and your partners want in on a B or C round? Or what about that entrepreneur's next company? Elman offers only encouragement as we say our good-byes.

"This is great. I want to lean in and talk to the team," he says, referring to others inside Greylock. "The last time we met," he tells the CEO, "I was seventy-five percent sure what you were proposing would work. Now I have a higher confidence range."

On the way to the next meeting, Elman gives me the arguments against investing, starting with the CEO himself. "If we were to invest, we'd have to have a difficult conversation about whether he would be the CEO moving forward," he says. The valuation was another possible deal killer—especially when the company's founder had just told him that they would probably lose their best engineers if forced to accept a down round.

"But for argument's sake," he says—and then proceeds to outline the opposing views:

Yes, the company has blown through a lot of money in search of a working business model, but it still has multiple millions in the bank. More important, he adds, "They finally have a winning story to tell." The company has been booking significant revenues, and all the numbers point in the right direction. "They're no longer scratching and clawing the way they were," he says. Maybe a fortyfold increase in revenues over the next eighteen months is on the giddy side of optimistic, but what if they grow twenty times? Elman does some quick calculations in his head and imagines a time in just a few years where, based on even these more modest growth numbers, the company is generating $300 million or more in annual revenues.

A big smile flashes on his face. "Then," he says, stopping to look at me, "it becomes interesting." Maybe he'd help them grow into a giant business. More likely, though, he says, "they sell to Facebook because Facebook will realize they need it." If they see the opportunity to book a few hundred million dollars a year in revenue, so would a Facebook or a Google.

The real question seems to be whether it would be worth the level of engagement that investing in the CEO's venture would demand. The potential is there for a threefold or fivefold or maybe tenfold return on their investment (ROI). But this is hardly an Instagram, where Greylock took part in a B-round investment at the start of 2012 and several weeks later collected on its share of the winnings when the company sold to Facebook for $1 billion. "One problem with this business is that it's the companies that aren't working out take up an inordinate amount of your time," Elman laments. "Those are the ones that sap your energy and your enthusiasm and your willingness to get into the next one."

We've reached our destination, which ends the conversation but also punctuates it. It's a portfolio company in which Elman has invested millions of Greylock's dollars. Yet in recent months, things haven't been going as expected. "They've hit a plateau," he says—a potentially fatal affliction to any venture-backed company.

2

VENTURE CAPITAL 101

Y ou've stumbled on a breakthrough idea with moun-
tainous moneymaking potential. To cash in on your
idea, you've created a company you're calling BigAssDeal.
com. Going to a bank to borrow money isn't an option.
Sure, that's what businesses large and small do to fund their
growth. But yours is an unproven concept in a nonexistent
market. It'll be months, if not years, before BigAssDeal
starts seeing any revenues. And without revenues, you can't
start repaying a loan. Go talk to a loan officer if you want,
but unless you're already rich, no bank will lend you the
cash you need.

Putting the business on a credit card is an option, albeit a limited one. You can buy ads on Google or Facebook
to drive traffic to your site. You can use plastic to hire the
overseas programmers who can help you build a prototype
on the cheap. But it'll cost you hundreds of thousands of

dollars, if not millions, to gain traction. Eventually you'll need to move out of that spare bedroom or dining room and start hiring the people you need in order to grow. That means leases and salaries and other expenses. That's where the venture capitalists come in.

The upside to venture capital is that there's no money to repay. The VC (or often a syndicate of two or more venture firms) buys a piece of your company: cash (typically in the millions of dollars) in exchange for an ownership stake. The downside is obvious: it's still your company, but you no longer own all of it. But an old expression in venture holds that it's better to own a smaller slice of a billion-dollar pie than 100 percent of a pie worth nothing. Mark Zuckerberg owned only around 20 percent of Facebook by the time it went public. But as of the start of 2018, he had a net worth of $76 billion.

Typically, there are "angels" before the venture capitalists get involved. Josh Elman is what's called an early-stage investor, yet invariably there's been at least one "seed round" before he invests in a company. The seed investors might include friends and family—the families of Bill Gates, Jeff Bezos, and Mark Zuckerberg, for instance, all earned many millions of dollars as early investors in start-ups that became, respectively, Microsoft, Amazon, and Facebook—but mainly they're those called angels.

Breaking in as an angel investor means, first, having the kind of money that lets you write checks typically in the $50,000 to $250,000 range for a small piece of a company that may ultimately be worth nothing. *Angel* is a term borrowed from Broadway, where it was coined to describe wealthy patrons who put up the money to stage a play. The Silicon Valley version is the tech tycoon from one generation who helps fund the next. A star German engineer from the 1980s, Andy Bechtolsheim, who cofounded the once great Sun Microsystems, met Google founders Larry Page and Sergey Brin before they had even officially launched a company. The $100,000 check he wrote as an angel investor in 1998 was worth, post-IPO, roughly $1.5 billion. A half-dozen years later, Peter Thiel, a cofounder of PayPal, led (meaning he put in more money than anyone else) a small group of Silicon Valley veterans investing in Facebook only a few months after Zuckerberg had launched a social network aimed at connecting classmates and friends. Thiel personally invested $500,000 in Facebook in 2004. Eight years later, after the company went public, his stake was worth more than $1 billion. Fellow

PayPaler Reid Hoffman was preoccupied with a new company he had cofounded called LinkedIn, but he threw in another $37,500—an investment that would be worth more than $100 million.

One difference between an angel investor and a venture capitalist is that a VC doesn't need to be independently wealthy. A VC invests mainly other people's money, not his or her own. Greylock Partners, for instance, has roughly thirty investors (mostly university endowments and big charitable foundations) whose money it invests in promising start-ups. A lot of firms promise investors that its partners will throw in a few million dollars of their own money when raising a new fund, as a sign of good faith ("skin in the game," as it's called), but even then, a firm will typically front the cash on behalf of new partners who don't have that kind of money.

These days there's a new species that is part VC and part angel: "super angels." Increasingly, they are another source of employment for the wannabe VC. The super angels are angel investors in that they focus on the seed round (though occasionally they might compete for a piece of an A or B round). But they're like venture capitalists in that they raise the money they invest from the same pool

of professional money managers (endowments, foundations, pension funds, insurance pools) and rich people as
VCs do. Hoffman, who joined Greylock in 2009, described
them as "micro-VCs" when we met at the company's Sand
Hill offices several years back. His colleague David Sze,
the firm's senior managing partner, preferred a term I
had used when asking them both about the phenomenon:
"venture capital lite." Back then, Greylock tried compet-
ing with all those Mini-Mes able to write checks for $1
million or more, which lets a start-up hold on to a greater
portion of its company longer—an existential threat to an
early-stage VC such as Greylock. "We've created our own
internal super angel fund," Hoffman told me. Why cede
that ground without a fight when those same entrepreneurs
would happily meet with them?

The big venture firms typically raise a new fund every
few years. The $575 million fund Greylock raised in 2009
had become $1 billion by the time Elman was promoted
from "principal" (a salaried employee who probably enjoys
a small taste of a fund's profits) to partner a few months before the firm announced its next fund, in 2014. A long list of
investors, it seemed, was eager to give money to a firm well
connected and smart enough to get in early on Facebook,

LinkedIn, Instagram, Dropbox, and Airbnb. This time the partners raised another $1 billion, giving Greylock $3.5 billion under management. The partners decided they were now too large to do angel investing.

Elman explained what had happened during my time shadowing him in the fall of 2017. They were winning meetings with the right founders but the time they were devoting didn't match the ownership stakes they were offered. "Each of us has only so much bandwidth," Elman said—and each company in a venture capitalist's orbit meant time spent tending to that investment. "It's gotten to the point with the hottest companies, there'll be a giant round with thirty or forty investors, and you're writing a check for fifty thousand dollars or a hundred thousand dollars that sums up to two and a half million or three million." VCs aim to buy a meaningful share of a start-up in exchange for their investment, but that $100,000 would buy Greylock only a minuscule fraction of a company. There are nine partners on Greylock's latest $1 billion fund, which means that, roughly speaking, each is responsible for investing nearly $100 million. That involves writing a lot of $50,000 and $100,000 checks. Other big firms that had declared they would compete at the angel level have also since retreated.

The VCs were pushed further upstream, and a new economics took hold, especially in the competition to own a piece of the hottest start-ups. As recently as the early 2000s, the typical A round entailed spending $1 million to $3 million to buy a 20 percent share of a company. Now that same ownership stake at the A round is going to require $5 million to $8 million or sometimes more. Similarly, B rounds are routinely in the range of $10 million to $20 million, and it's not unusual to see checks twice that size. At those prices, Elman said, "We want to see some proof of concept, some momentum, before we invest." More than 95 percent of Greylock's investments are in the A or B rounds.

"We look for start-ups at that pivotal moment when they try to multiply from thirty people to a thousand people," Elman explained.

Those who invest after early-stage firms such as Elman's are generally called "growth-stage" or "late-stage" venture capitalists. Later rounds mean spending greater sums of money in exchange for a smaller share of a company—less risk but also less reward. For instance, the biggest winners in Uber are its angel investors, who put up the least money but will see the greatest multiples on the amounts they invested. That includes a super angel named Chris Sacca of Lowercase Capital, whose hits have also included Twitter, Instagram, and Kickstarter. Other big winners include Benchmark Capital, which headed an $11 million A round in 2011, and Menlo Ventures, which led a $37 million B round later that same year. But plenty of others playing the venture game are seeing big profits on Uber, at least on paper.

Uber is unusual because rather than raising capital by going public, like most tech companies of its size and success, it remained private long after it could have. So there have been not just C and D rounds but also E, F, and G. At each step, participants have seen their investment appreciate in value for this company valued at more than $68 billion at the end of 2017. A $363 million C round for roughly a 9 percent stake in the company is good news for Google Ventures, the venture fund that Google created in 2009 and that is now known simply by its initials, GV; Texas Pacific Group, or TPG, a giant of the private equity world; and also Shawn Carter, the rap artist and entrepreneur better known as Jay-Z. Their combined 9 percent share of Uber is worth, on paper, more than fifteen times what it was at the time of their investments. A year later, Fidelity

Investments was among those putting up money for a $1.4 billion D round that bought the mutual fund colossus and other investors roughly a 7.5 percent share in the company. And in 2015 a Connecticut-based hedge fund led a $1 billion E round that secured a 2.5 percent share of the company. Microsoft was the big investor five months later in a $1 billion round that locked up less than 2 percent of the company. Then in 2016 Saudi Arabia's Public Investment Fund, a sovereign wealth fund that invests on behalf of the government, picked up most of a $3.5 billion G round that bought it a 6 percent share of Uber.

Venture is all about exits. A company goes public, or it is bought. Otherwise there's not the "liquidity event" (turning a paper investment into cash) that allows VCs to disburse their share of the profits to investors. The hope of the Saudis, Microsoft, and every investor before them is that Uber will go public soon and attain a market cap in the hundreds of billions of dollars. Then they will have made an enviable threefold or fourfold return on their investment compared with the tenfold or so amount that a Fidelity would enjoy. In that scenario, Benchmark—the first venture money in Uber—will approach the fabled thousandfold ROI, while Lowercase and Chris Sacca (who worked at Google before becoming an angel investor) will own shares worth in the multiple billions on a stake he bought for $1 million or $2 million: a return rate far exceeding 1,000 percent.

IT'S THE RARE INVESTMENT that pays anywhere near that kind of payout, of course. Those are the "home runs" and "grand slams," as VCs describe them. More common even among early-stage investors are the winners that earn a firm three or five or ten times its money—"singles" or "doubles," in VC-speak. Even the industry's stars fail roughly two-thirds of the time, just as the very best in baseball do, and every VC has his or her share of embarrassing strikeouts. It's an occupational hazard in an industry where the biggest fear isn't costing your partnership millions of dollars on a bad investment but knowing you said no when you had a chance to get in early on a great one such as Facebook.

"You know from experience that there are all these risks you didn't think about before making an investment," said Maha Ibrahim, a longtime partner at Canaan Partners, an early-stage venture fund with offices on both the East and

West Coasts. Ibrahim had become a VC in March 2000, just as the air was starting to rush out of the dot-com bubble. Her first investment, in a mobile credit card reader start-up, taught her that being too early with a new technology can sometimes be as bad as being too late. "I blew twelve million dollars on that deal," she recalled, "but that's venture capital. You know the fifty ways an investment can go south, but you're still putting millions—sometimes tens of millions—into a company, knowing that there's a good chance it won't work."

That's what's scary about being a venture capitalist and also what makes it so fascinating a world. "This is a business about risk," Ibrahim observed. "The people who are rewarded are the ones who stick their neck out, not the people happy in the pack." The braver the VC, the dumber he or she is likely to look after making a mistake. "Part of being a VC is the risk of making a really stupid investment," she said.

Even the best VCs can be wrong—sometimes spectacularly so. A few years back, there was all this hype about a company called Juicero, which was peddling a $699 juicer. Never mind the absurd price (the "price point," in VC-speak) for a home appliance being described as a Wi-Fi–connected juice press or that Bloomberg proved the juicer (by then marked down to $399) was essentially useless when a reporter was able to squeeze the fruit packs just as effectively with her bare hands. The founder had no experience running a tech company, and his claim to fame was a juice bar chain (Organic Avenue) that had gone bankrupt. Yet the angels poured $4 million into Juicero in 2013, and the venture capitalists followed with a $16.5 million A round six months later. Subsequent B and C rounds brought in nearly $100 million more. In all, Juicero raised $118.5 million in venture dollars before announcing in September 2017 that it was ceasing operations. Among the victims: venerable Kleiner Perkins and Google Ventures. Between them, they burned through tens of millions of dollars backing a company that was losing $4 million a month when the investors pulled the plug.

"This is a business where you miss more than you hit," said Ted Schlein, a partner at Kleiner since the mid-1990s. "You get used to that, or you find another line of work."

As CAREERS GO, VENTURE can seem an enviable one. Like Hollywood casting directors, VCs spend part of most days dressed casually, sitting around a conference table and sipping bottled water, auditioning entrepreneurs one hour at a time. The typical firm will invest in fifteen to twenty firms a year—the best of the best. "Every day means spending time with smart, creative people working on these incredible ideas," Josh Elman said. Is it any wonder that twenty-eight-year-old Nikhil Basu Trivedi at Shasta Ventures describes himself as "blessed"? He's in meetings constantly, he said, "but it's who you're spending time with that matters." There's usually something extraordinary even about the entrepreneurs whose companies they don't fund. "It's interesting to meet with entrepreneurs who are dreaming up the next big thing," Basu Trivedi said. It helps that he works at a top-tier firms whose recent hits include Dollar Shave Club, which Unilever bought for $1 billion in 2016, and Nest Labs, a maker of "smart" home devices such as thermostats and alarm systems that Google bought for $3.2 billion in 2014.

The money is a big draw. In theory, VCs are like the entrepreneurs they back: they grow rich only if enough of the companies in which they invest flourish. In reality, today's venture capitalists are so well compensated on the front end that the only question is whether they end up rich or crazy rich. The key to a VC's wealth is the "carry": the percentage of the winnings that the partners take before distributing the profits to their investors. Twenty percent is standard, but top firms such as Greylock take a 25 percent or 30 percent share. So for every $100 million generated in profits, the partners take a $20 million to $30 million cut before distributing the rest among their investors. Meanwhile, there's also the "management fee" of 2 percent or 2.5 percent that venture capital firms charge their investors. In the case of a billion-dollar fund, that works out to another $20 million to $25 million. There's also what might be called the layering factor: the big firms raise a new fund every two to four years, yet funds typically charge these fees over five years. That means the more successful firms are simultaneously collecting management fees on two or three funds, plus their shares of the carries.

At top firms, the lowest associate slogging through the slush piles of pitches and poring over the financials of would-be portfolio companies pulls down somewhere between $120,000 and $150,000 a year. A promotion to junior VC—a principal at some companies; a "venture partner" at others—translates into an annual salary closer to $500,000, along with a nibble of the carry. The general partners at the more established firms make an annual salary of $1 million or more, but that's only a fraction of the money they hope to pocket. A partner at a top Valley firm told me that he and his partners paid themselves $3 million apiece every year. Surprised by a figure that high, I blurted out, "But I thought most of your money is from the carry?"

"It is," he said, offering a shrug and an apologetic smile. On the condition that I not name him or his firm, he walked me through the math. At his shop, they take a 30 percent cut before distributing profits. "The aim on an early-stage fund is five x," he said: $5 billion on a $1 billion fund, or $4 billion in profits. (Late-growth VCs hope for something closer to a threefold return.) In that scenario, he and his half-dozen or so partners will split $1.2 billion (30 percent of the profits) over the life of that one fund. A successful VC for a top-tier firm can expect to earn somewhere between $10 million and $20 million a year. The very best make even more. John Doerr is in a category all his own, with a net worth above $7 billion, but Mike Moritz and Doug Leone, longtime partners at Sequoia Capital, another storied Silicon Valley firm, both have a net worth in the $3 billion range. So does Jim Breyer, who for years was the managing partner at Accel Partners (now just Accel). Accel was the first venture money in Facebook: the $12.7 million it invested in 2005 was worth roughly $10 billion after the social network's 2012 IPO. Helping to boost Breyer's bottom line was the $1 million of his personal wealth that he invested alongside Accel—a stake valued at more than $1 billion after Facebook's public offering.

Most everyone who has attained any kind of success in Silicon Valley seems to dream of becoming a venture capitalist. "I have the same experience over and over," said Scott Dettmer, a Palo Alto–based attorney who in 1995 cofounded Gunderson Dettmer, a law firm that caters to fast-growth tech start-ups. "A founder sells his company, he takes a few months off, and then he's asking for an appointment to visit. And that's when he tells me he wants to be a venture capitalist. I take a deep breath. 'Okay, let's talk about it. Let's make sure you really want that.'" Invariably, Dettmer said, they do.

"I came up in an era where for entrepreneurs, for everyone I knew, being a VC was aspirational," said Keith Rabois, a partner at Khosla Ventures. Rabois, who was twenty-six years old when Netscape went public, worked as a lawyer for a few years before taking a job as a deal maker for PayPal, the company founded by his college friend Peter Thiel, along with Max Levchin and Elon Musk. There Rabois worked alongside Reid Hoffman, another member of what came to be widely known as the "PayPal Mafia," given the remarkable success of people who worked there (including a creator of YouTube, a cofounder of Yelp, and a producer of the 2005 movie *Thank You for Smoking*). eBay bought PayPal for $1.5 billion in 2002, and Rabois took a job with Hoffman, who had founded LinkedIn shortly after PayPal's sale. Rabois's résumé would include stints at Slide (founded by Levchin and sold to Google in 2010 for $182 million) and also Square, a mobile payments company that today is a publicly traded company worth $35 billion. Meanwhile, Rabois used some of the sizable payoffs he had received as an early employee at both PayPal and LinkedIn to play angel investor to dozens of companies. Rabois left Square at the start of 2013 in the wake of sexual harassment allegations that he denied (the alleged victim was a male employee), but his track record as an angel investor was such (LinkedIn, Airbnb, Yelp, Lyft) that within two months he was working at Khosla Ventures.

"Becoming a venture capitalist has always been a goal," said Rabois, who turned forty-eight in 2017. The wider world might venerate the entrepreneur, but for many successful entrepreneurs, the dream is life as a working venture capitalist. "People put the entrepreneur on top, but where does the entrepreneur go? Up and down Sand Hill Road, chasing money. Everyone looks up to the VCs."

Reid Hoffman and Peter Thiel, two of Silicon Valley's more celebrated entrepreneurs, became venture capitalists. Thiel joined the ranks of the VCs almost immediately after selling PayPal to eBay, when he created what he called the Founders Fund. As Thiel explained for me in 2006 over drinks at the Four Seasons in San Francisco, where he was living at the time, the change in direction stemmed from something of a lifestyle choice. "When you're doing a next company, you're focused very narrowly and intensely on this one thing," he said. "As opposed to when you're a venture capitalist. I'm exposed every day to all these brilliant people who have brilliant ideas from all these different areas." Hoffman followed him into venture when he joined Greylock Partners seven years after starting LinkedIn. "There's something about helping entrepreneurs grow their companies that I find invigorating," he said.

YET VENTURE IS NOT right for everyone. For starters, it's a hard job—much harder than it might seem from the outside. "I really thought when I joined this business, I could put my feet up on the desk, and the distributions would be automatically sent to my bank account," a VC named Nick Sturiale told me years ago. Sturiale had cofounded a company and then worked in product development or marketing at several start-ups before joining the well-regarded Sevin Rosen Funds. "I've worked as hard being a VC as I did on any start-up," he said. "The myth of venture capital being a lifestyle utopia is just that: a myth." (Sturiale is now a managing partner at Ignition Partners, a firm specializing in early-stage business software start-ups.) Keith Rabois figures he sees around ten to twenty new companies every week. "It's extremely exhausting," he said, but he also feels he has no choice but to push himself that hard. "This business is mostly about not missing out on the next amazing company," he explained. "So you make that next meeting and the one after that, no matter how exhausted you feel."

"Doing venture is what I thought I'd do when I was ready to retire," said Andrew Beebe, a serial entrepreneur who joined Obvious Ventures in 2015. "I'm not saying that I'm working harder than I ever have, but it's hard fucking work." Adding to the stresses is that Obvious is a newer firm, which makes fund-raising that much more challenging. "We just raised a second fund, which was no easy task when we've only been around a few years," Beebe said. That's another downside to working as a venture capitalist, according to Max Levchin. "The part I could never get my head around," he said, "is that you have to work relentlessly for ten years just to determine if you're any good at the job."

Levchin has founded or cofounded seven companies, including, most recently, Affirm, an online lender that was valued at $1.5 billion at the end of 2017. Yet even one of the Valley's more acclaimed serial entrepreneurs confessed that he, too, dreams of becoming a VC. "Any time I've been between companies, I've thought, 'Okay, this is the time I'm going to go be a venture capitalist,'" he told me when we met at Affirm's San Francisco offices in 2017. "In venture, your brain is churning all day long with the potential of all these ideas. I love brainstorming; I love hanging out with a bunch of smart people. Instead of putting all your energy into this one narrow thing."

Yet Levchin recognized he wasn't venture capital material. He had practically birthed Yelp in his offices in the mid-2000s and provided the online rating service with its early seed money—and then felt he was the "helicopter parent" that no entrepreneurial venture needs early in its life. "I remember very distinctly a moment when I thought, 'Why don't you get out the way and let me drive this car now?'" he confessed. "I was becoming the investor no entrepreneur wants: the guy everyone is wishing would stop with advice and unwanted help." Levchin had a similar experience after providing seed money to the founders of Pinterest, the digital scrapbook site. "I'm self-aware enough to know I'm clearly too tactile to be a venture capitalist," Levchin said. "I really want to be the one doing the building and not offering advice from the sideline."

Working as a venture capitalist demands being hyper-social, whether you're built that way or not. Maha Ibrahim confesses that she's not innately gregarious. Ibrahim, who earned her PhD in economics from the Massachusetts Institute of Technology (MIT) in 1997, originally imagined herself living the relatively isolated life of a university professor. But she was lured into the business world by the remarkable tech breakthroughs going on all around her. "I'm not an extrovert," she jokes, "but I play one in real life." She needs to be "on" every time an entrepreneur comes to her office soliciting funding, and hers is a job that requires deep working relationships with a wide range of people—from the executives at the companies she funds to the VCs at other firms—who are her competition but also sometimes her partners on other investments. "I go home and collapse at the end of some days," she said. "I don't want to talk to anyone and just want to be alone."

Josh Elman might want to just be a dad watching his daughter play soccer on a Saturday, but he's also a VC working for one of the area's top venture firms. Occasionally, that means engaging on the sidelines with founders who feel like they've just run into the candy man. "The scary thing is that how you handle every encounter determines how you are perceived," he said. "What I say to that parent [at a soccer game], or how I handle myself during every meeting. You have one person saying, 'He was looking at his phone the whole time,' 'He wasn't even paying attention,' and that can really mess up your reputation." Venture companies these days hire public relations firms to help build their brand, but Elman is convinced that what he calls "the whisper network" counts ten times more than a firm's public reputation or any good will a VC builds via blog posts or media interviews. "This industry works on an entrepreneur saying, 'Josh Elman is great! You really need to go meet Josh.'"

Being a VC also means bracing yourself for the humility of being wrong a lot of the time and also getting beat. "You have to learn to live with uncertainty, not just in relation to the outside world but also internally, with your partners and in your own head," Ibrahim reflected. Failure is part of the job. You lose investments to a rival. Or you win but then wish you hadn't. A start-up may gain traction, but then a larger company appropriates the idea, and you can only watch as it uses the reach of its installed base to crush your portfolio company.

Then there's the heartbreak of what VCs call the "living dead." These are companies that are modestly profitable but not prosperous enough to go public or to attract a potential buyer. Invariably, they drain a lot of your energy over the years, and even though they might generate a couple of million dollars annually in profits, they are a nuisance: a bookkeeping hassle for funds that have a life span of seven to ten years.

The work can be isolating, too. "It's a pretty solo existence," Elman said. "You have partners, but each of us ends up with our own portfolios. Each of us is out there trying to find our own companies though our own network. For a lot of people, I think their attitude would be, 'You know,

I'd rather have a regular job and be part of a team rather than off on my own like this.' You really have to want to be a VC." Being a VC also involves spending a lot of time delivering disappointing news. "People might get jaded by having to say no all the time," Nikhil Basu Trivedi said. The high-risk nature of the business might also prove frustrating to some. "You see a lot of companies and people you care about fail," he added.

"When people tell me they want to be a VC, I really push them," Maha Ibrahim said. "I ask, 'Do you really have the passion?' 'Are you really built to be a VC?' 'Are you just drawn to shiny objects, or are you thesis driven and have a thoughtful approach to the marketplace?' I ask them hard questions, and if they still answer yes, I say, 'Just network the hell out of it, and hopefully an opening will come about.'" Her only other tip is that venture funds tend to hire associates in the spring.

Josh Elman finds himself becoming rabbinical whenever friends and friends of friends tell him they want to become a venture capitalist. He repeats an old story about a non-Jew approaching a rabbi about wanting to convert to Judaism. "The rabbi is like, 'No, you don't,' and then gives a hundred reasons why you don't want to be Jewish. 'Have you ever had bacon or a cheeseburger? Well, that'll be the end of that. You ever watch football on Saturdays? No more.'" The rabbi rebuffs the potential convert a second time and maybe even a third before taking the person seriously. "You really have to want it," Elman said.

3

A QUICK HISTORY OF VENTURE CAPITAL

It's always good to know a little about a profession if you're trying it on for size. The history of venture capital begins after World War II. Before then, there were just rich people who invested in promising-sounding ventures. For instance, J. P. Morgan, the famous banker who came to prominence in the late 1800s, financed railroad companies and other outside industrial endeavors early in the twentieth century. In the 1920s, Cornelius Vanderbilt provided seed capital to the founder of Pan-American Airways. In the 1930s, J. H. Whitney funded motion picture studios, and Laurance Rockefeller, a US Navy pilot, helped finance the growth of Eastern Air Lines and the McDonnell Aircraft Corporation, which became McDonnell Douglas and then part of Boeing, the world's largest aircraft manufacturer. During World War II, the US Army chose the Florida Foods Corporation to create a powdered orange juice for its troops, and Vanderbilt put up the money. The war ended before the product was ready for mass distribution, but the company continued operations and ultimately renamed itself the Minute Maid Corporation.

Georges Doriot is widely considered to be the first full-time professional venture capitalist. Born in France, he earned an MBA at Harvard Business School and then, in 1946, raised $5 million, largely from insurance companies and wealthy individuals. The resulting company, the American Research and Development Corporation, would make any number of smart investments in fledgling businesses but none more farsighted than Digital Equipment Corporation (DEC). The $70,000 that Doriot invested in DEC in 1957 was worth more than $350 million when the company went public in 1968—a return roughly five thousand times its initial investment. Stated differently, that initial $70,000 provided a rate of return of more than 100 percent per year.

Two of Doriot's disciples, along with a third man, ventured off on their own in 1965, when they raised $10 million from a half-dozen wealthy families and individuals. The trio opened an office in Cambridge, Massachusetts, and called their firm Greylock Partners. Greylock's early hits included Wang Laboratories, an early PC maker that, at its peak, employed more than 30,000 people; Brookstone, the high-end gadget store; Neutrogena, a giant in the health and beauty sector; and Teradyne, an equipment-testing company that is today worth $8 billion.

In Palo Alto, the Hewlett-Packard Company was gaining attention as a maker of test equipment and other electronics. Hewlett-Packard's going public in 1957 drew attention to the West Coast tech scene. Just weeks before, the Soviet Union had launched Sputnik, the first satellite to orbit the earth, provoking Cold War–era fears that the Soviets—then the world's other great nuclear superpower—had gained a leg up on America. The Russians' beating America into space spurred Congress to pass the Small Business Investment Act of 1958, which made federal dollars available for the funding of small independent businesses. That same year, the Department of Defense established the Defense Advanced Research Projects Administration, or DARPA, opening the floodgates for government funding of a wide array of new technologies, including, ultimately, the internet. One year later, William Henry Draper Jr., an East

Coast banker who had also served as undersecretary of the army, opened what is widely believed to be California's first venture firm, Draper, Gaither, and Anderson. Draper's son and later his grandson and great-granddaughter would get into the business.

The area's first star—the VC who put West Coast venture capital on the map—was Arthur Rock. The son of candy store owners from upstate New York, Rock was another Wall Street refugee with an MBA from Harvard when he arrived in San Francisco in 1961. Rock was an early investor in the Intel Corporation in 1968 and then, a decade later, in Apple.

Don Valentine was also an original Apple investor. The son of a truck driver, Valentine was a gruff, straight-talking sales executive from New York who worked in the chip (semiconductor) industry. Success as an angel investor inspired him to raise money from several wealthy people, and in 1972 he founded Sequoia Capital, maybe the most incredible venture firm ever created. His first investment was in the pioneering video-game maker Atari, where Steve Jobs had gone to work after dropping out of Reed College. "Steve was un-degreed, some people said unwashed, and he looked like Ho Chi Minh," Valentine said, referring to the wispy-bearded Communist revolutionary who served as president of North Vietnam for more than forty years, from the end of World War II until his death at the height of the Vietnam War in 1969. But he recognized Jobs as brilliant and a visionary, if not also a difficult character, and the check that Sequoia wrote in 1977 to help fund Apple was for $150,000—more than twice as much as the one written by Arthur Rock. Over the next decade, Sequoia was also an early investor in Oracle Corporation, Cisco Systems, and Electronic Arts (EA).

There must have been something about 1972. That same year Eugene Kleiner, a founder of Fairchild Semiconductor Corporation (a precursor of Intel), and Tom Perkins, an early Hewlett-Packard executive, founded Kleiner Perkins. (The firm added two more partners over the next few years and changed its name to Kleiner Perkins Caufield & Byers.) Its first megahit was Genentech, a biotech company founded in 1976 on the premise that manipulating human DNA offered opportunities to mass market therapeutic products. (Genentech, which went public in 1980, was bought in 2009 by the Swiss health care company Roche for $47 billion.) Kleiner was also an early investor in EA, as well as in Compaq Computer (an early giant of the PC world),

Symantec Corporation, Intuit, and Sun Microsystems. Several of those investments were championed by John Doerr, a twenty-nine-year-old Intel computer chip salesman (though one with a master's in electrical engineering and an MBA from Harvard) whom the firm added to its roster in 1980. "They wanted a gofer to help check out new business plans," Doerr said. He took the job because he thought one day he might want to create his own company, and Kleiner "promised that if I worked for them, they would someday back me in starting a new venture."

IN VENTURE THERE ARE the "GPs" (general partners) and the "LPs" (limited partners). The GPs are the salaried partners who make the investment decisions, while the LPs are the fund's investors. In the early years of venture capital, that meant wealthy people, but eventually others discovered the lure of these funds that held the promise of astronomical returns. University endowments began investing in venture, in no small part because it's the very rich who sit on the board of trustees of any prestigious university, and they saw firsthand its moneymaking potential. They were followed by other so-called institutional investors: the professional money managers who oversee multibillion-dollar pools of money for big charitable foundations, insurance companies, and others. A key inflection point was a change in the rules in the late 1970s that opened venture capital to pension funds. In 1978 the country's venture capitalists collectively raised $218 million. By 1983, they had raised $3.6 billion.

"It used to be that you had two or three months" to decide about investing in a company, Eugene Kleiner told the *Wall Street Journal* in the early 1980s. "Now it's a matter of weeks or even days, because if we don't, somebody else will."

The PC age was dawning, and with it a need for software and peripherals. Venture has always been about more than just technology companies, but in the first half of the 1980s, that's where the big money was to be made. David Marquardt was thirty years old, with a degree in mechanical engineering from Columbia University and a newly minted Stanford MBA, when in 1980 he cofounded Technology Venture Investors. Not long afterward, he heard about "Billy Gates" and a small software concern called Microsoft. Marquardt invested $1 million in Microsoft in exchange for a 5 percent share of the company. A dozen years later, that stake was worth $15 billion, or a $1.5 million profit on every $100 invested.

Sevin Rosen was another of the dozens of new firms that opened offices on Sand Hill Road. Its investments over the coming decade included Compaq, Silicon Graphics (Steven Spielberg used its machines to breathe life into the dinosaurs that populate the *Jurassic Park* movies), and Lotus Development Corporation (the maker of the first popular spreadsheet program, a forerunner of Excel). "It was a very good time to be a venture capitalist," the firm's cofounder, Ben Rosen, told me years later when I visited him at his sprawling Central Park West apartment with floor-to-ceiling windows that offered spectacular views of the park and the Manhattan skyline. For much of the interview, I was fixated by the miniaturized private jet just over one shoulder as we spoke—tossed in free by the manufacturer, he explained, when buying an aircraft that had cost around $20 million.

Not every venture firm generates private-jet profits. Not every year is a good one in the venture business. The standard measure of success in venture is the *internal rate of return*, or IRR, for each fund a firm raises. That's a way of expressing the annual return a fund produces during its lifetime. The average venture fund raised in 1982—a "vintage" 1982 fund, as if a bottle of wine—had an IRR of just under 33 percent a year, which meant investors were practically doubling their money every two years. Yet the average IRR dropped to under 10 percent by the late 1980s. The $5 billion a year that was flowing into venture in the mid-1980s barely cracked $3 billion in 1991.

The Netscape IPO in 1995 represented what a venture capitalist might call a proof point: evidence that a fledgling company that was only one or two years old can cash out—go public—long before it is profitable, so long as investors believe that by purchasing stock shares they are taking an ownership stake in the future. Venture raised $10 billion in 1996, $20 billion in 1997, and another $26 billion in 1998, and the competition to own a piece of a hot deal grew even more fierce. During this period, I spent the better part of a month hanging around with Tim Draper, the grandson of California's first venture capitalist and son of another pioneering VC, and his partner, John Fisher, whom Draper had met when both were working as junior investment bankers. "I saw one of the traditionally conservative firms make an offer to an entrepreneur at the end of a first meeting," Fisher told me. "No follow-up calls. No checking of references. Just an offer of one million dollars on the spot for a piece of their company." Among the worst culprits? He and Draper, Fisher confessed. "We were slapping down bets as fast as we could," he said.

A venture capitalist named Kathryn Gould was among those who believed that some of her colleagues had lost their senses. Gould had become a venture capitalist in the late 1980s after a successful stint running marketing at Oracle. She was still one of the rare women in venture when, in 1995, she cofounded her own firm, Foundation Capital. By investing primarily in lesser-known business software enterprises, she attained a personal lifetime IRR, she claimed, of 90 percent a year. (Gould passed away in 2015.) She seemed almost offended by most of the business pitches her firm was receiving in the second half of the 1990s. "They're coming in saying they're going public within eighteen months," she told me back then. "Either that or they're building something that Yahoo!, or AOL, or whoever would be buying in a year for twenty million." All pretenses of building a great company had been dropped. Yet with so much money sloshing around, slapping a ".com" at the end of a business's name almost guaranteed that an entrepreneur with a half-decent idea could gain funding. In the first half of the 1990s, the VCs were backing an average of two thousand companies a year. That swelled to just under eight thousand in 1999 and more than twelve thousand in 2000.

Venture dollars don't grow on trees. But for a time in the second half of the 1990s, it seemed as if they did. Venture firms raised $58 billion in 1999 and another $101 billion in 2000. "We had people coming to our office—people we had never met—saying, 'I want to put five million in your next fund,'" Draper recalled. That was the story at every top-tier venture firm. Existing LPs were upping the percentage of their capital they were dedicating to venture capital, and new ones were clamoring to get in. Money rained down on the venture world: from Europe, from Japan, from the scores of established enterprises that created a corporate venture arm, including tech giants such as Intel and Hewlett-Packard. "We simply won't rest," a firm called OffRoad Capital Corporation vowed cheekily, "until we give the country's excluded millionaires the pre-public-investment access they so rightfully deserve."

The second half of the 1990s also saw the rise of the super angel, pioneered by Ron Conway, a longtime tech veteran who seemed an unlikely champion for a newly hatched internet company. An assistant printed out his emails and then typed in Conway's handwritten responses. But few in Silicon Valley were better connected. In 1998 Conway raised $30 million for Angel Investors I, and then, because demand was so great, he raised five times that amount for Angel Investors II. Like any VC, he charged an annual management fee and took his 20 percent cut before distributing profits to his investors, who included some of the Valley's best-known figures as well as Tiger Woods, Arnold Schwarzenegger, Henry Kissinger, and Shaquille O'Neal.

A correction was inevitable. According to the National Venture Capital Association, the number of venture firms had swollen from 183 in 1995 to more than 1,000 by the end of the decade. The ranks of venture capitalists more than doubled during that same period: from fewer than five thousand VCs in 1995 to nearly ten thousand by 2000. More venture-backed enterprises meant more companies clamoring to go public, and there seemed no limit to investors' appetites for anything tech related. (From the cover of *Newsweek*: "The Whine of '99. Everyone's Getting Rich but Me!") These days, there might be an average of one or two IPOs a week. The last three months of 1999 brought more than two a day. "The internet is the greatest legal creation of wealth in the history of the planet," John Doerr famously told any reporter within earshot, including me. I thought it was a clever, if historically dubious, statement. Soon, however, it would sound more like an admission of guilt.

The dot-com bubble didn't pop so much as deflate over an eighteen-month period beginning in early 2000. One measure of the madness had been the astronomical rise of the tech-heavy Nasdaq composite index. An index that began 1995 below 1,000 crossed 5,000 in March 2000. By April, the Nasdaq had dropped by more than 20 percent— and kept falling. Thousands of companies had been funded assuming a quick strike (the mantra then: "Grow big fast or go home"), but the public markets had snapped shut. And most of the same young upstarts funded with tens of millions of venture dollars, assuming they would soon be worth billions, ended up going out of business. By October 2002, the Nasdaq had lost nearly 80 percent of its value. More than a dozen years passed before the Nasdaq again surpassed 5,000, in 2015.

It wasn't all bad news for LPs. Those who had invested in a venture firm early in the dot-com boom were richly rewarded. The vintage 1995 funds ended up producing (when calculated ten years later) an average IRR of 42 percent, according to the consulting firm Cambridge Associates. At that rate, LPs were doubling their money every two years. Funds raised in 1996 produced an average IRR of 37 percent, and those in the top quartile (the top 25 percent) generated an annualized profit of 81 percent. Funds raised in 1997 provided okay returns—10 percent a year—but the 1998, 1999, and 2000 vintages were big losers. Firms ranked in the bottom quartile lost 11 percent a year on funds raised in 1999—at that rate, a $1 million investment would be worth $312,000 a decade later—but the top firms also disappointed investors. Even venture outfits in the top quartile generated an annualized return of merely 4 percent—barely enough to cover the yearly management fees investors paid.

Angel Investor I, the maiden fund raised by super angel Ron Conway, generated better returns than other vintage 1998 funds. But Angel Investor II, which closed at the end of 1999, was more typical. Nearly every start-up in the Angel Investor II portfolio went out of business not long after the dot-com crash—nearly two hundred in all—but Conway had also muscled his way into the Google deal. ("Ron is the premier elbow guy in the business," Conway's partner had told me at the time.) That was venture capital encapsulated: a couple of hundred worthless investments, but a single big hit that makes up for a lot of mistakes. "If you held on to your Google stock for any length of time," one Conway LP told me, "you actually ended up doing very well on Angel II."

ONE FALLOUT OF THE dot-com bust was the temporary death of what venture capitalists call the "consumer space": shorthand for internet start-ups selling to the wider public rather than to other businesses. "You saw it up and down Sand Hill Road," said Tod Francis, the managing partner at the well-regarded Shasta Ventures, where Nikhil Basu Trivedi went to work in 2012. "Almost universally, venture firms said, 'You know, we're not comfortable working with consumer stuff; we're really a technology- and engineering-based industry. We made a mistake going into these consumer businesses, and we promise never to do it again.'"

That was Andrew Anker's experience at August Capital, another top-echelon firm. Anker, a former investment banker who had spent the previous four years as *Wired* magazine's chief technology officer, joined in August 1999. "I was brought in as the 'consumer guy,'" he said. He led the firm's investments in the social planning website Evite, Listen.com (a precursor of Spotify), and Ebates, the online coupon concern, that a Japanese company would buy for $1 billion. But after the dot-com crash, Anker said, "I was told in no uncertain terms by my partners, 'We don't want to do consumer right now and maybe never will again.'" He brought potentially interesting deals to his partners (including one he would invest in personally "and make a bunch of cash"), but they rejected them all. One partner told him, "I would sooner predict the movement of an atom than the purchasing behavior of a consumer." Out of frustration, Anker left the partnership in 2003.

The dot-com crash caused the exit of any number of VCs. Unlike Anker, most did not leave voluntarily. "The tourist VCs"—that's what those in the industry any length of time derisively called the newcomers who had invaded their ranks, and there was a sense of good riddance once they were gone. So much competition had led to inflation-ary prices and less time for thoughtful contemplation and proper due diligence. "We tend to like it when things get depressed," Kleiner's Ted Schlein said. "Dips mean better prices and less competition."

Problems lingered. All that money in the hands of the venture capitalists when everything came crashing down meant a problem that banker types call "overhang," which invokes (as I wrote when reporting on the state of venture for *Wired* in 2003) "cash so plentiful that tree branches sprouting $1,000 bills groan from the weight." With so much capital on hand, start-ups were being kept on life sup-port by firms willing to fund B and C rounds because what else were they going to do with that money? Just maybe, one investment would be the one Google that saves the port-folio. Average IRRs remained under 10 percent for several more years. Fund-raising dipped again after the 2008–09 financial crisis, but that might have been a positive from the perspective of an industry where too much money in the hands of too many VCs causes problems.

The trauma of the late 1990s left in its wake lingering fears of another bubble. There were warnings that the sky was again falling in the early 2000s, when a few intrepid souls among the tech VCs invested in fledgling social media start-ups, and then again in the middle of the decade, after Google went public and valuations began to soar. More recently, worries have been voiced loudly about the plethora of "unicorns"—techtalk for start-ups valued at more than $1 billion—and the return of inflationary prices to the venture world.

Yet the naysayers once declared absurd the $5 million Kleiner Perkins paid in 1994 for roughly a quarter of Netscape—an investment worth more than $400 million barely one year later. Similarly, doubters were plentiful when Kleiner and Sequoia spent $25 million between them to buy 10 percent each in Google. Search was a mature business, the critics offered. Others warned about a company being run by two PhDs. Yet KP's ownership stake in Google was eventually worth multiple billions of dollars. Ditto the $12.2 million Accel paid for a piece of Facebook. That's venture capital, a sport played best by risk takers who understand that the cost of getting into a deal doesn't matter nearly as much as the price that the next person up the food chain—whether a larger company or investors through an IPO—is willing to pay.

"We always have lots of little bubbles in Silicon Valley," observed Paul Saffo, a tech forecaster and one of the area's better-known pundits. "It's like the froth on cappuccino. A little froth is a very good thing. A lot of froth, especially if you mix in a lot of inexperienced people, that's a bad thing."

4

LAYING PIPE

Josh Elman never set out to be a venture capitalist. He was the accidental VC who, until he was twenty-nine years old, had never for a moment thought about becoming a venture capitalist. That might be the best way to become one. Allen Morgan spent seventeen years as a start-up lawyer in Silicon Valley before, in 1998, joining the Mayfield Fund, a top-tier firm for which he had done legal work. "When I'm approached by young people who ask me, 'How do I get into venture?' what I usually say is 'Go be wildly successful at something else first,'" he said. Better yet, according to Morgan, now semiretired and a self-described "Sherpa" to young start-ups, "go be a product person"— a product manager or the like—"at a successful company. That's the best way to break into venture nowadays."

Tod Francis of Shasta Ventures offers more or less the same advice, albeit with an extra layer of analysis. Francis tells wannabe VCs that there are two basic routes into the industry. One is the "apprentice" path: start off in a junior role at a venture firm and learn by working closely with its investing partners. The other is what he and others call the "ops," or operations, route: make your name at one or more hot tech companies before seeking to join a venture firm. That's the far more popular path into venture these days, Francis says, and also the route that Elman took.

Elman, who grew up in the Seattle area, arrived in the San Francisco Bay Area at the start of the internet era, in 1993, when he attended Stanford. There his major was symbolic systems, which, he was quick to tell me, was also Reid Hoffman's major. "It's a combination of linguistics, psychology, philosophy, and computer science," Elman explained. "The idea is to study how people think and how computers think—to sort of bridge that interaction." He interned for a summer at Microsoft and worked another summer for an internet start-up called Homestead Technologies, which Intuit bought a decade later for $170 million. "At that point, I was completely naïve about venture and funding," he said.

After graduating, Elman returned to Seattle, seeking work at a "prepublic company." He thought about taking a job at Amazon, which was then a three-year-old online company that sold mainly books, but preferred another young Seattle company called Progressive Networks. Founded by a former Microsoft executive named Rob Glaser, its goal was a programmer's dream: to better deliver sound and video over the web. "To my mind, there really wasn't any choice: this place selling books except over the internet versus audio and video," Elman said. A cousin worked there and helped him secure an interview and, ultimately, a job.

The company changed its name to RealNetworks in 1997, the same year that Elman began as a programmer there. He worked on the company's RealJukebox, which let users "rip" their CDs, transforming them into MP3 files that could be listened to over a computer. Three years after starting at RealNetworks, Elman said, he was managing fifteen or so engineers working on a Microsoft Windows version of RealPlayer. "Hundreds of millions of users using our products, and I wrote a bunch of the code," Elman said. "It was an incredible first job." He was just twenty-four years old.

There were frustrations, however. At its peak, Real-Networks had 250 million users. The company pioneered streaming media of all kinds, from music to radio to movies. "RealNetworks truly could've been Netflix or YouTube or iTunes or Spotify. Or all of them," Elman said. He saw the mistakes the company was making and wasn't shy about sharing his views. "I would go to meetings with people on the business side, and they're telling me why we need to do this feature or make this change," he recalled. For instance, in order to boost revenues, why not deliver an ad every time a user fired up RealPlayer?

"I told them, 'That's gonna piss off all our users, and there's not going to be any revenue when everyone jumps to other players,'" he said. But they had MBAs and could read a spreadsheet, and he couldn't. "They'd be like, 'You're just a little engineer; we're in product development, we make these decisions.' That's when I realized I needed an MBA." In the fall of 2003, Elman returned to the Bay Area to start classes at the University of California at Berkeley's Haas School of Business.

"I quickly learned two things," Elman said. "One is that actually I learned a lot of what I wanted to in one semester: how to read a cash flow statement, how to read an accounting statement for a company's balance sheet—things that are obvious if you went through a finance program but not obvious if you'd come up in engineering and programming." The other thing he discovered in those first weeks on campus was that many of his classmates were there "so they could graduate and run a product that hundreds of millions of people were using. And I thought, 'Wait a sec: Why am I in business school if the job I'm gonna get is so similar to the one I just left?'" It was also during that first semester that Elman learned about the role the venture capitalist plays in the start-up ecosystem. "A classmate is telling me how he wants to be an entrepreneur, and I just blurted it out," Elman said. "I was like, 'You know what? Now that I finally understand a little about what they do, maybe I wanna be a VC someday.'"

Silicon Valley was just emerging from the nuclear winter that followed the fission of the dot-com bubble. Social networking was starting to become a big deal in the fall of 2003. Friendster, a predecessor of Facebook, had recently raised millions in venture financing, as had LinkedIn. Elman was only a few months into a two-year program, but he emailed jobs@friendster.com. He heard nothing from Friendster, but, through a Stanford career board, he saw a listing for a Windows programmer at LinkedIn. "Here I was a good Windows programmer and very interested in social networking," Elman said. "So I wrote to them and said, 'Hey, if I could help you guys at all, I would love to.'" He mentioned that he was in graduate school with a goal of becoming a product manager—a job outside the engineering track. "They write back to me and say, 'Come here and be a product manager,'" Elman said.

Elman had gotten married by that point, and his wife worked in Cupertino, which was fifty miles south of Berkeley. They had chosen to live in a mutually inconvenient spot roughly halfway between the two, ensuring that both husband and wife were spending too much time in traffic. And LinkedIn's offices were conveniently located in Mountain View, only a few miles from Cupertino. "It's January, this was literally the first or second week of the second semester. I did a lot of fretting before deciding to drop out," Elman recalled. Officials at the school essentially mocked his decision. "This one administrator tells me, 'Everybody but one person who dropped out in the dot-com bubble came back to finish their MBA. You'll be back in two to three years.'" Even the professor who taught entrepreneurship at the school was dubious. "He tells me, 'Social networking will never work,'" Elman said.

LinkedIn had only around fifteen employees when Elman began working there in early 2004. The company had recently closed on a $4.7 million A round, led by Sequoia, and was in the midst of a hiring spree. Elman's job as product manager was largely about finding ways to drive users to the LinkedIn site. He spent his days running endless "A/B tests"—trying things two different ways and seeing which proved the more effective approach. "It was at LinkedIn where I finally understood, 'Okay, this is how you actually do business in the world,'" Elman said. "It's there I learned what it was to be a product manager and not an engineer."

Not that he felt he really fit in at LinkedIn. "I was going to all these HR and recruiting conferences and not really liking it," he said. "And as much as I believed LinkedIn was going to be a multibillion-dollar company, I wasn't loving working in jobs and recruiting." It also wasn't the start-up experience as he'd imagined it. "LinkedIn is immensely successful, but even in the early days, people didn't stay late in the office," Elman said. Reid Hoffman was already in his thirties when he created LinkedIn, as were several of his cofounders. Yet rather than be glad that he had found a job that left room for a balanced life, Elman felt shortchanged.

"I felt jealous of friends who were working late every night and feeling like they were changing the world," he said. "That sounded a lot more fun than what I was doing. So I asked myself, 'Why aren't I at a company like that?' I let myself start looking around a little bit."

———

As the senior partner at Shasta, Tod Francis plays a role closer to firm ambassador. These days he spends more time playing nice with the LPs than working the vineyards in search of new companies, along with other tasks he's taken on so that his younger colleagues aren't distracted. "I'm talking all the time at schools and business schools, and it's always the same question: 'How do I get into venture?'" Francis said. So often has he been asked that question in his twenty-five years as a VC that he's practically written up a class lecture on the topic. "I've literally written out the pros and cons of venture, why you'd want to do it, why you wouldn't," Francis said. "But all they really want to hear is how to get in."

Francis tells his own origin story, of course. Like Elman, he decided he wanted to be a VC while earning his MBA. Francis went to Northwestern University's Kellogg School of Management, where one of his professors was a working VC. "He tells me I'd have to work for at least ten years before his firm would even talk to me," Francis said. So he spent ten years out in the work world, first at Johnson & Johnson as a marketing manager for the Tylenol line shortly after a series of poisonings in 1982. Seven people in the Chicago area died because an unknown person or persons placed cyanide-laced tablets in bottles of Extra-Strength Tylenol, forcing the company to pull every bottle off the shelves nationally. Four years later, he moved to a consulting firm that let him spend the next half-dozen years jobbing out its marketing and other branding services to start-ups. In the early 1990s, he was offered a position as an associate at Trinity Ventures, a Sand Hill firm famous for having funded Starbucks.

"I thought it was going to be a two-year play because that's what I was told by the firm when I joined," Francis said. "My wife said, 'Well, if you're good, they'll wanna keep you,' but I kept saying, 'You don't understand the model, you don't understand the model.' Well, stuff happens. Someone left the firm, and they needed a consumer guy, and I got my shot." While at Trinity, Francis worked on investments in Jamba Juice, P. F. Chang's, the Wedding Channel, and the BabyCenter, a dot-com era idea for a site that would serve the need of every new parent. In 2003 he joined Shasta Ventures, where his recent investments include TaskRabbit (hire people to take care of everyday tasks), Mint (a personal finance site), and Liquid Space (a marketplace for flexible office space).

The "ops" route today looks different from when Francis was younger, starting with the kind of company where a job applicant should seek employment. "I tell people wanting to take the ops route, 'Start with a large company,' because at a large company they can train you, you can make mistakes, and it doesn't hurt the company at all," Francis advised. Yet by "large," he doesn't mean a Johnson & Johnson, where he started, or a General Motors or even a Microsoft. "Today it might mean joining Uber," he said. "Maybe it meant joining Facebook three years ago, or PayPal before that, or eBay. There's all these really good people there you can learn from. You can learn just by watching good operating principles take place. And, without realizing it, you're building your network for the future."

Sometimes a single hit, if big enough, might suffice. The venture ranks are thick with people who made their bones—their reputations—at a Google or a Microsoft. For most, though, there are still at least a couple of more steps. "I tell people, 'Go be part of an early-stage company,'" Francis said. He might as well have been describing Elman's life. Seventeen months after starting at LinkedIn, Elman jumped to Zazzle, a Kleiner-backed start-up that lets people slap an image (a wedding photo, a snapshot of a child) on everything from stamps to T-shirts to coffee mugs.

"Reid was like, 'I'm going to make sure that the LinkedIn shares you're leaving on the table are worth more than what you're picking up at Zazzle,'" Elman said. "My response was, 'I bet you Zazzle can do it!' Wrong." Whereas Microsoft bought LinkedIn for $26 billion in 2016, Zazzle, more than a decade after it was founded, and despite raising $60 million in venture capital, never provided the big strike. Though profitable, the company is what another VC might call the walking dead. "I thought on-demand commerce could be massive and Zazzle would be the company," he reflected. "It turned out that on-demand *custom* commerce is not that massive."

Francis knows better than most the odds against making a big strike in the venture game. "The good news is that the start-up you go work for doesn't necessarily have to be successful," he said. "It doesn't matter that Josh went to a company that failed, or at least didn't make it big. The established high-growth company already gives you the credibility. He's still the guy out of LinkedIn." In other words, even a failed start-up gives you a story to tell. "That start-up that flames out lets you say, 'Yeah, well, here's what I learned working in a start-up, and here's how I and we screwed up,' " Francis said.

Those seeking to put together a golden résumé to wow a future venture firm, Francis said, need to have made a name for themselves working for a big-name A or B round start-up. "The ideal version would be someone succeeding in a high-profile role at a high-growth company that might be doing twenty million dollars in revenue and looking to go to one hundred million," Francis said. That could have been LinkedIn, but Elman had left there too early to make any claims. "This was 2007, 2008, and LinkedIn was getting pretty huge," Elman said. Zazzle, in contrast, underwent a massive hiring spree followed by mass firings, "and then it was basically me and the founders [a father and his two sons] and the college crew that had been with the brothers from the start." Elman added the obvious: "There were times when I was like, 'Maybe I should have stayed [at LinkedIn].' "

Elman had been at Zazzle for around two and a half years when he was stopped for speeding twice in a month. "That was kind of a sign to me that I was a little bit overly stressed and taking too much on personally," he said. "My rule is, everyone gets a speeding ticket every once in a while. But once you get one, you're paying more attention. I wasn't paying attention."

Elman thought about venture at that point. He had made it a point to get to know Greylock's David Sze after Sze led a $10 million B round in LinkedIn in 2005. Conveniently, Sze had sought him out not long after Elman had started at Zazzle. "A bunch of people left LinkedIn around the time I left, and, as an investor, he was concerned," Elman said. "He had invested all this money in the company and wanted to know 'Why are people that we think are good people jumping ship?'" The two had kept in touch, but Elman knew it was premature to make his bid to join a firm as a venture capitalist

"I didn't feel like I was even close to qualified," Elman admitted. "When I looked at venture capitalists back then, they had been executives and founders. Or they had an MBA, finished their MBA program, and either came from an investment background or maybe had been true executives somewhere. I had been close to an executive at Zazzle, but it's not like it was even this really successful company that everyone was talking about. I didn't feel like I was there yet."

Josh Elman has never heard Francis's lecture, but he

might as well have been following it. At the end of 2007, he compiled a list of companies where he thought he might want to work. He put Facebook on top. "I was convinced Facebook was going to win and knew I'd love to be part of it," he said. This was four years before Mark Zuckerberg's company went public, and few people had any idea how massive its potential was. (Facebook is now one of five or six companies worldwide with a market cap above $500 billion.) "I started thinking, 'Okay, if I can get an interesting job at Facebook working on their social platform and make that really successful, and then Facebook goes public and gets really big, after I do something meaningful there, maybe I can make my case to be a VC,'" Elman said. He started at Facebook in early 2008.

If Elman has a criticism of his résumé, it's that he jumped around too much. Francis talks of two or three stops when building up the perfect résumé with which to impress a VC. Elman, at that point, had worked for three companies—four if you include RealNetworks. He had worked at LinkedIn for less than two years and left Zazzle several months before his third anniversary there. And again he was feeling restless. "I'm more of a product guy, and at Facebook most of my job was talking to third parties, trying to get them to use the platform," he said. He was happy to have done it—"I learned a lot and built up a lot of skills," he said—but also eager to leave. After nineteen months at Facebook, he took a job as a product manager at Twitter.

"I was like, 'I'm gonna ride Twitter as long as I can,'" Elman said. "I'm going be at Twitter for five or six years, I'm going to build a bunch of stuff, experience the IPO, and stay around for a few years. Then, when I'm ready to come up . . ." He didn't finish his sentence, but he didn't have to. No matter how busy he was, he continued, he always took the time to meet with a VC if the opportunity presented itself. "I'd be at some event occasionally, and whenever a VC would say, "Hey, could you help a company of ours?' I would always meet with them and help them any way I could."

Elman had a big job inside Twitter. "They basically said to me when I was hired, 'Everybody signs up for Twitter, but not enough people stick around. Help us fix that.' That was kind of my mission from Ev"—Evan Williams, a Twitter cofounder and the company's CEO when Elman was hired. His job, in other words, was to grow the user base. Elman founded and ran a new team that focused on engagement and retention. The company reached more than a hundred million active users during his tenure. "The Twitter job was absolutely perfect—for a year," he said."

Elman had been at Twitter just twelve months when the company announced that it was replacing Williams as CEO. A month or two after Williams was out, so was the company's longtime vice president of product. Company cofounder Jack Dorsey returned to the company around this point. "Everything changed after that," Elman said. "Dorsey comes back, and he's kind of leading product. He and I didn't click, and I got fired three months later." In July 2011 he found himself unemployed and left to figure out what to do next.

AT FIRST, ELMAN CHOSE to be coy about his intentions after his high-profile firing. He met with every VC who contacted him, but invariably they were reaching out to interest him in going to work for one of their portfolio companies. "I had the same answer for everybody. I was like, 'No, I don't want anything right now,'" he said. What he wouldn't say was that he was looking to become a VC—at least until emboldened after a conversation with Mark Sus-

ter, a partner in a Los Angeles–based VC firm called GRP
Partners (now Upfront Ventures).

"Mark gave me great advice," Elman said. "He told me,
'If you think you wanna try to be a VC, you have to *tell*
people you wanna be a VC.'" After that, he let people know
of his interest. "They'd be like, 'Oh, cool! We're not really
hiring, but here's some friends who are,' and then I'd meet
with them," he said.

Elman thought about reaching out to either David Sze
at Greylock or Reid Hoffman, who had joined the firm in
2009. "I put it off because they were my first choice," Elman
explained. Better he should experience some dry runs with
others, he rationalized, while he was still figuring out everything. Right around the time he was feeling ready to
reach out to Sze or Hoffman, he received an email from a
third partner at the firm, James Slavet, who proposed that
the two meet for coffee. "James was one of the VCs who
would occasionally ask me to help one of his companies,"
Elman said.

The two met for a coffee at a café in Palo Alto, not far
from Sand Hill Road. "I tell him point-blank I want to be
a VC, and he says, 'Great, because we're looking to hire a
principal,'" Elman said. He was being offered a job if he

wanted it. The catch? It was that it was a two-year posting that would likely end up as part of the executive team with a company that Greylock hoped would grow huge. Elman only had to look at the person whose place he was taking to realize that his odds of ever making partner at Greylock were dim. David Thacker had earned his MBA at Harvard and spent five years at Google, where he had been a product manager for AdWords, Google's flagship advertising product. In addition, he had built the company's product team in Europe. Yet Thacker and his golden résumé spent just over two years at Greylock before he left to join Groupon as a vice president, shortly after the partners invested in the online coupon company at the start of 2011.

Slavet was nothing if not blunt with Elman. "He tells me, 'You can come join for a couple of years, learn a lot about becoming a VC, and then find a great company to jump in as a senior,'" Elman recalled. "He says, 'Honestly, very few people make it to partner, so don't expect that.'" And in case Elman missed the point, Slavet put the odds of his making partner at 1 percent. Nevertheless, said Elman, "I wanted to learn from great people, and I wanted to figure out if being a VC was even for me. I knew I had to take the chance."

———

THE GREYLOCK WAY HAD always been to hire the best and brightest out of Harvard Business School and teach them the business by teaming them up with the firm's senior partners. For decades, the company had exemplified the apprentice method.

David Sze was one of the first exceptions when he was hired as a partner in 2000. Sze had attended Yale University as an undergrad and earned his MBA, though at Stanford rather than at Harvard. His résumé after that read as if following the playbook that Tod Francis would later draft. Sze spent thirteen months as a junior product manager at Electronic Arts, which by then was already a rising giant in the video-game market, and then moved to a smaller, high-growth gaming company called Crystal Dynamics.

Netscape went public in the summer of 1995. Tod Francis counsels prospective VCs to stay at a company long enough to reasonably take ownership of some element of its success but also to be flexible enough to jump when the right opportunity presents itself. Sze, eager to work for an internet company, left Crystal Dynamics after only two years when offered a position as marketing director at a company called

Architext. Shortly after Sze went to work there, his new employer changed its name to Excite, which became an early, internet 1.0 star. For a time, Excite and Yahoo! competed to become the web's dominant "portal": a user-friendly place for people to create a personal home page, complete with a search bar and customizable components such as news, sports, weather, and entertaining tidbits.

In 1999, at the peak of the dot-com mania, @Home bought Excite (both Kleiner Perkins–backed companies) for $6.7 billion. Sze was named senior vice president of product strategy for the new company, but he got lucky: Greylock, a venerable East Coast firm, wanted to build a consumer internet practice and recognized that it needed more of a West Coast presence if it were to compete to get into deals there. Sze had already started as a partner at Greylock in 2000, two years before Excite@Home declared bankruptcy. He was in his midthirties.

John Doerr once cracked famously that a VC isn't seasoned until he or she has crashed the equivalent of an F/A-18 fighter jet. "It takes probably six to eight years," he once told me, "and you should be prepared for losses of about twenty million dollars." (Doerr's own Waterloo had almost been a company called GO Corporation, which failed so spectacularly and blew through so much cash that *Startup: A Silicon Valley Adventure*, a book about the disaster written by its founder, Jerry Kaplan, is a cult classic.) Sze was Greylock's second hire for its West Coast outpost. The first had been Aneel Bhusri, a top executive at a Bay Area–based business software giant called PeopleSoft (later bought by Oracle for $10 billion), also with an MBA from Stanford rather than Harvard.

That was 1999, which might have been the worst moment in history to start as a venture capitalist. In an interview with *Bloomberg Businessweek*, Bhusri confessed to losing roughly $70 million in his eighteen months as a VC. That included what the magazine described as "dot-com duds like CameraWorld.com, Guru.com, and an online rewards network called HelloAsia. (The office joke: 'HelloAsia, goodbye $15 million.')"

Sze's investment in LinkedIn went a long way toward wiping out any losses the West Coast racked up while learning the venture game. It also helped build Greylock's reputation as a Silicon Valley powerhouse. Often, a successful venture boils down to recognizing a company's potential when others don't, but sometimes it's simply a matter of beating out the competition for a piece of a hot deal. Reid

Hoffman had his choice of investors in the early days of LinkedIn. "It never occurred to me to go and pitch Greylock," he confessed later. But then he met Sze and saw in him and Greylock a partner that could help him grow the company. "David talked about LinkedIn in a way that was totally different from everyone else I was meeting," Hoffman said. Greylock invested $10 million in LinkedIn in 2004—a stake worth $1.2 billion on the day LinkedIn went public in 2011.

In part because of his investment in LinkedIn, Sze was on a short list of firms that Facebook was looking to pitch in 2005. "I had a chance to look at it," Sze would admit years later in an interview with *Newsweek*, but he "turned it down because I was working on closing another deal." He was given a second chance a year later in a B round that valued Facebook at a little more than $500 million. (It's now worth roughly a thousand times that.) Some of his partners felt that they were overpaying for a piece of an unproven company whose competition included Friendster and the then popular MySpace. But Sze convinced them of Facebook's potential to move beyond college campuses and connect people of all ages. The firm paid roughly $12.5 million for approximately 2 percent of Facebook in 2006. A half-dozen years later, that stake would be worth more than $2 billion on the day the company went public.

In 2009 Greylock announced it was moving its headquarters to Sand Hill Road. Soon half the firm's Boston partners were out. "Fundamentally, Silicon Valley has created a culture of 'Nothing is impossible,'" the managing partner at the time explained. "Boston has lost some of that."

Forbes would cite Sze's Facebook and LinkedIn wins when ranking him fourth on its 2012 Midas List, as well as Greylock's 14 percent stake in Pandora, which also went public in 2011. Sze would again make the top ten in 2012, by which point his fellow West Coast pioneer Aneel Bhusri had made the list three times—including an eighth-place showing in 2009 for investments in start-ups looking to conquer less publicized areas of tech such as data storage and cloud computing. (Bhusri is now the CEO of Workday, a publicly traded company worth $28 billion, and an advisor to Greylock.) James Slavet, who had first recruited Elman, was among the other Greylock partners to make the Midas List. Reid Hoffman ranked third in 2011 for his investment in Airbnb, among other successes.

THE LIFE OF THE JUNIOR VC is not an easy one. Wesley Chan, a thirty-nine-year-old partner at Felicis Ventures, a relatively new Valley firm focused on early-stage consumer start-ups (Shopify, Dollar Shave Club, and Fitbit, a leader of wearable technologies that was worth $10 billion shortly after its 2015 IPO), has seen the toll it's taken on friends and colleagues. Initially, they feel like they've been offered their dream job. But after a year or two, they are miserable. "I have one friend who joined this great, great firm after a wonderful career as an operator," Chan said. "A real star at what he had been doing but wants to try his hand at being a VC. He's written two checks so far, and they're both in companies just piddling along. He's in his second year, still looking to do that one big deal, and freaking out that he's blowing it."

Chan was fortunate. Following a stint as an early tech star at Google, he'd then helped launch its venture firm, Google Ventures, where he spent four-plus years. In 2014 Felicis hired him as a general partner. With sympathy, he has watched those he knows who are invited to join a firm as a principal, an associate, an investing partner—or whatever the firm calls its junior VCs—floundering a year or eighteen months into the job.

Chan mentions another friend in the business who calls it the "death spiral." "That's his term for when you're in the second or third year, where you start losing confidence that you'll ever find the company you're looking for, so you start getting more desperate," he explained. "You write more checks just to get more shots on goal." During the death spiral, the junior VC makes matters worse for the partners by investing in lousy companies "just because you feel pressure to get more deals done before your two or three years." Adding to the stresses, Chan said, is that a junior VC's success depends a lot on factors beyond his or her control. "At the end of the day, you're also at the mercy of the partner that you're apprenticing with," he said. "If he sucks, you're screwed. If he's the type who doesn't give credit, you're screwed. You're imagining this wonderful career in venture, but until you've proven yourself, it's a lot of anxieties."

Elman had heard similar stories. To minimize the pressure he felt, he lowered the stakes. "I told myself that maybe I'll discover that Greylock is not the place for me. Or maybe I won't like being a VC," he said. "Or I like being a VC but find another firm that's just as good. Basically, I figured, 'Best case, I become a VC at Greylock, but if not, I could live with the options.'" Now that he had some distance from the unpleasantness of his final months at Twitter, he could even imagine going back to work for a young, high-growth start-up.

"The longer I was away from Twitter, the more I began to think about the mistakes I made that got me fired," he said candidly. "I could've been a better employee through a time of transition instead of an aggressive one trying to push things that I believed were right, which created more chaos in the company." A part of him felt cheated out of the start-up experience he had been seeking since having dropped out of business school. He had joined Twitter for "a ride on the rocket ship" and the thrill of an IPO. Instead, he'd been fired after less than two years.

"The thing I discovered about myself is that I'm a second-wave guy," Elman said. "I can come into chaos and help get a bunch of stuff moving. I'm able to recognize the signal through the noise of an early-stage company." That's a good trait for a venture capitalist but also an invaluable skill in an ecosystem crowded with early-stage tech start-ups eager to strike it rich. "I can drive traffic and get a company to where it's doubling and tripling and quadrupling revenue," Elman said. He hoped he would make it as a VC—but, if not, "I welcomed another shot at being a better employee this time around and staying through an IPO and beyond."

Some people chafe in a job with no real power. Elman, though, found his lack of decision-making power liberating. "They were actually pretty clear about it: 'You are not a partner. You're not leading investments,'" he said. "So, to my mind, the pressure was off. I told myself my job was to find great companies that I believe Greylock should invest in, and then try to convince a partner at Greylock to step up and lead that investment. But if a deal didn't get done, I knew I had done my job by getting us to think about it seriously as a firm."

Elman spent his first weeks as a venture capitalist taking a lot of meetings in cafés dotted around the Bay Area. A truism of venture is that an investor's best opportunities aren't unsolicited pitches that arrive via email but those discovered while working your network. "Venture is fundamentally a networking business," David Sze explained. "It's how you get into venture, and it's how you become successful as a venture capitalist." On that front, Elman's job-hopping proved advantageous: in jumping from LinkedIn, to Zazzle, to Facebook, to Twitter, he had met and worked with that many more talented engineers and product people. He spread the word in his network that he was looking for interesting projects and reunited with former colleagues who were suddenly long-lost friends happy to sit down with someone from Greylock, even if only a scout. The partners were also a source of deal flow. "They would say, 'Hey, I don't have time to meet this one—go meet them,'" Elman said. "And then my job was to build a relationship with that company."

"Laying pipe"—that's one expression I've heard people in venture use for building their network. One VC spoke about "laying down bricks," as if his job were constructing pathways to send deals his way. Whatever the preferred term, the VC's life is a social one, whether that of a newbie or a ten-year veteran. "You go to conferences," Elman said. "You go to evening meetings. Every time I was invited to speak about growth and the lessons I learned from LinkedIn and Twitter and Facebook, I said yes." In the early days especially, he said, "I was going to events all the time. Meeting lots of entrepreneurs and other VCs." He spent a lot of his time as a junior VC meeting with angel investors, who were another critical source of potential deals.

"People would ask me, 'Can you sit down with this company?'" Elman said. "It didn't make a difference that I had no connection to the company. I would always say yes. I'd go help them with growth and try to turn it into a potential investor conversation."

Venture is typically a buyer's market. Greylock, as the buyer, hears thousands of business pitches a year yet funds less than two dozen of them. Yet venture is sometimes a seller's market in which the entrepreneurs have their pick of funders. Word spreads that a repeat entrepreneur with a strong track record is at work on a stealth project. Or an angel-backed start-up is a supernova lighting up the sky. "On those deals where an entrepreneur can have his choice of VCs, the question you've got to answer is 'Why you?'" says Tod Francis. "Why will an entrepreneur choose you over the other five people they're gonna meet with that day?"

Venture capitalists take the measure of founders, but they are simultaneously being sized up themselves—and the successful VC needs a persuasive sales spiel to woo entrepreneurs who have their choice of suitors.

Here Elman saw himself as having a competitive edge. For starters, he is an engineer. "It's changed some over the last few years, but when I started in 2011, 2012, it was rare to have VCs with deep product experience," he said. "David

Sze was one of the very few in his generation with a core role in product management, and while it's more common today, I was kind of this vanguard in my generation." He also could talk about LinkedIn, Facebook, and Twitter. "The fact that I had all these experiences made the conversations a lot more credible, even when I was brand new to venture," Elman said. He would contrast himself with the other associates and principals "running around with an MBA or some lighter background and who hadn't had that depth of operational experience." He sold himself as a "second-wave guy" to first-wave founders eager to get to where LinkedIn and Facebook and Twitter had gotten.

"There are people who can stay and scale and scale and scale companies until they're massive," Elman said. "They're big-company people. But there are others like me who really get the start-up chaos but aren't the kind who can scale to the point of massive—we actually make good VC candidates."

Early-stage venture capitalists generally declare a focus area: cloud computing, say, or platforms and networks. Elman chose as his area the consumer internet, which is probably the most competitive specialty area. The firm's website listed him as an investor, describing him as interested in "social networks and platforms, mobile apps, and new media and marketplaces." He announced on LinkedIn that he was a principal at Greylock and declared himself "most excited about big visions from people who want to change the world."

Elman worked at avoiding what VCs sometimes call "happy ears." That's when virtually every company sounds like a possible winner. "It doesn't help anyone if every company you meet, you're like, 'We should do this deal! We should do this deal!'" he said. "Because you're not being a filter." The other failure scenario has new VCs talking themselves out of every possible investment. "The success formula is that you get good at serving up deals that everyone will find interesting," Elman said. "I was just doing as much as I could to make sure I could bring the few companies I was actually excited about to the partners."

Several weeks before Elman began working there, Greylock had finalized a $4.9 million B round in Whosay, a New York–based start-up selling a suite of services for big-name businesses and celebs wanting to manage an online presence across platforms. David Sze, who led the investment in Whosay, took Elman to his first board meeting with the company. "I had just come from a run of social media companies, so the idea was to get me involved as they managed growth," Elman explained. He was named a "board observer," which let him attend Whosay's board meetings as a nonvoting member. McDonald's, Coca-Cola, and Macy's were among the well-known brands signing up for Whosay before the company was sold at the start of 2018 to Viacom (the owner of MTV, Nickelodeon, Comedy Central, and Paramount Pictures) for an undisclosed amount of money.

Elman played a similar role at Nextdoor—eventually. Nextdoor was a closed social network that allowed neighbors to communicate with one another in private. Once again, David Sze had "sourced" the deal, Elman said, but this time, when he suggested that Elman sit in on board meetings as an observer, the firm's cofounder and CEO, Nirav Tolia, said no. However, when the two met to talk, Tolia broached the idea of Elman's leaving Greylock for Nextdoor. "He says, 'You have the right background; maybe you could work for me,'" Elman said. "I told him, 'Look, I'm trying this VC thing. I might get to stick around Greylock longer, maybe I won't, but for now, Greylock is an investor in your company. How can I help?'" In effect, Elman became a kind of part-time consultant to the firm. "I'd go there every week and spend a couple of hours with their product team, teaching them some of the stuff I'd learned through my experience and helping them through some issues around growth," he said. "At some point, Nirav said, 'Hey, maybe Josh can start joining the board meetings.'"

If Elman had any trepidation when starting as a VC, it was that he'd never been a founder or a CEO and therefore had never sat on a company's board of directors. "I was always insecure about being a board member," he admitted. His experience with Nextdoor helped cure him of that. "Getting invited into the boardroom that way was both a signal to me—and I think to David, too. Like, 'Maybe Josh really can add strategic value,'" Elman said. Every new VC, including Elman, focused on finding new companies, true. But equally important, from the perspective of his bosses, was an ability to help the firm's portfolio companies. "Because if you think about it," he said, "part of the bet on a VC as a partner is not just whether they're gonna be a good investor, but also are they gonna be a good steward of the capital we invest."

ELMAN HAD BEEN ON the job around a year and was still a junior VC when a friend told him about a start-up in Southern

California called Snapchat. The friend had been a frat brother with the founders and offered to make an introduction. "A lot of the job is serendipity," Elman said. He first spoke with the founders on the phone and then met with them when they were in the Bay Area. "I was wowed," he recalled. "I probably pounded on the table harder for Snap than for any other company." He recognized, however, that a disappearing photo app wouldn't be the easiest sell. "But venture capital is about believing that things that can sound crazy or stupid right now have the potential to change the world," he said.

Greylock's partners decided against investing in Snapchat. Instead, Benchmark Capital led a $13.5 million A round in early 2013 that included Silicon Valley Angels, a network of high-net-worth individuals, and Lightspeed Venture Partners, an early-stage venture firm that had picked up most of Snap's $485,000 seed round several months earlier. Still, Elman remained close to the company, including its CEO and cofounder, Evan Spiegel.

"Not long after they close the A round, Evan says to me, 'Hey, I'm thinking about raising more money; we'd like to have you guys involved,'" Elman said. Several times, he flew to Los Angeles to visit with Spiegel and his team, as the partners considered an investment more seriously. But

Greylock recently had invested in another messaging app start-up, which spooked Spiegel, as did the reality that his contact at the firm might not even be there in a year. In June Institutional Venture Partners, a long-time Valley-based firm, carried the largest share of an $80 million B round that included the Boston-based venture firm General Catalyst—but not Greylock.

"That was sort of the moment where the team running Greylock basically started saying, 'Well, maybe he should be a partner,'" Elman said. In July 2013, one month after Snapchat closed its B round, he was elevated to full partner. Only later, in the winter of 2017, when Snapchat went public, could Elman's partners calculate the size of their mistake. Benchmark owned 12.9 percent of a company worth $28 billion at the end of its first day of trading—a stake worth more than $3.5 billion. Missing out on the B round, Elman said, "ended up being a half-a-billion-dollar mistake. But that's venture and how much a single miss can cost."

ELMAN DIDN'T WASTE MUCH time. In November, just four months after becoming a full partner, he closed his first deal: co-leading a $12.5 million A round in the start-up

SmartThings, which made hardware and software that connected home appliances to the internet. Two months later, he led a pair of investments, both involving start-ups that allowed him to take advantage of his former Twitter ties.

One was Jelly, a new kind of search engine based on crowdsourcing and being built by a team headed by Twitter cofounder Biz Stone. Its investors prior to Greylock included former vice president Al Gore, fellow Twitter cofounder Jack Dorsey, and super angel Ron Conway. Elman took a board seat at Jelly in 2014 after orchestrating a B round for an undisclosed amount.

Elman's other Twitter-related investment is also probably his highest profile: Medium, the online publishing platform founded by his old boss Evan Williams. "I made sure to catch up with Ev for coffee every three to six months 'cause I knew he was working on something interesting, and I wanted to be able to fund him," Elman said. "If I hadn't done that, he might not have called us at the right time." Greylock conducted a $25 million A round in Medium alongside several well-known angel investors (including the ubiquitous Ron Conway) and Hollywood mogul Michael Ovitz. Since that time, Elman and his partners have watched the company's valuation swell as other big-name

investors, including Andreessen Horowitz (cofounded by
Marc Andreessen of Netscape fame) and Google Ventures,
have invested another $100-plus million in subsequent B
and C rounds. "I feel really lucky that Ev called us when he
was deciding to raise money," Elman said.

Elman would make another half-dozen investments over
the next several years. They included Operator, an online marketplace curated by experts, and Life on Air, the
company behind Meerkat, a phone app that let users live-
broadcast video. Meerkat was a sensation in 2015, after wow-
ing the audience gathered in Austin, Texas, that year for
the South by Southwest festival—and dead a year later after
Twitter launched Periscope, "a strikingly similar competi-
tor built mostly in stealth mode," the website TechCrunch
reported, and bought for "nearly $100 million." Meerkat
was still riding high when Elman led a crowded $14 mil-
lion B round investment that listed twenty-two other investors, including YouTube cocreator Chad Hurley and CAA
Ventures, an early-stage fund created by the talent agency
Creative Artists Agency. At that point, Life on Air had to
"pivot," in VC-speak, and thus was born Houseparty, which
its CEO envisions serving as "the internet's living room"
(imagine a video version of a chat room). Another was El-

man's 2015 investment in Discord, a chat and messaging tool for online gamers.

A common complaint among newer VCs is the lack of feedback from the marketplace. They continue writing multimillion-dollar checks even as they have little concrete idea of what the investments they've already made might be worth. "I can't stop making investments and say, 'Okay, let's wait seven or ten years so I can learn and see what I should've done differently,'" said Keith Rabois, a venture capitalist since 2013. "You keep making investments because that's your job."

Elman was luckier than most. Ten months after his very first investment in SmartThings, Samsung Electronics bought the company for $200 million—a solid single in his first at-bat that earned Greylock around five times its investment. There would be several more modest wins over the next few years. Pinterest bought Jelly in March 2017 (the deal terms were not announced), and Elman would score another quick hit on a company called Musical.ly, a social network for creating and sharing short video clips. Greylock was one of several venture firms taking part in a $16.6 million B round in Musical.ly in August 2015, and then threw in more cash as part of a $130 million C round the following May, when the company was valued at just over $500 million. In November 2017 the Beijing-based company Toutiao bought Musical.ly for $800 million.

Yet Elman also experienced his first flameout not long after news of the Musical.ly buyout. Citing the success of SmartThings, Elman, in mid-2015, led a B round investment in Otto, a start-up in San Mateo, California. The company was working on a digital lock that would allow users to remotely lock and unlock their doors. Its product was handsome and well crafted ("Imagine if a Swiss watch and a Volvo had a love child," said the company's CEO) but pricey at $700—not including the $150 installation charge. In December 2017 Otto ceased operations without ever having brought a product to market. Venture capital is about the start-ups you miss out on but also, Elman said, "about the regrets when things don't go as you'd hoped."

A NEW VC SPENDS most of his or her time hunting for new investments. More seasoned venture partners split their time between finding new start-ups and helping ones in which they have already invested. This past fall, when I spent time with Elman, he had been a venture capitalist for more than six years and a full partner for just over four. At that point, he was sitting on a half-dozen boards. And he was surprised that he was spending as much time—if not more in some weeks—helping companies that Greylock had already funded as he was searching out new ones.

"At Greylock, helping the entrepreneur is like our religion," Elman said. "It doesn't matter whether the entrepreneur is someone we're backing, or in a company in which we're considering an investment, or whether we're just meeting casually for the first time—you're doing what you can to help that person." That obligation increases exponentially for the VC who has led an investment in a company. "If I'm a member of the board, the burden is on me to do whatever I can to help the founders succeed," he said. "The burden is on me to find the best possible return for the shareholders in that company and the employees and everyone else involved."

In October I join Elman for a visit to one of his portfolio companies. After months of rapid growth, the start-up has stalled, and the VC is there to better understand why and to brainstorm potential solutions. First, however, there is a small mess that needs cleaning up: Elman and the CEO have inadvertently angered a large, potentially important corporate partner, so much of the hourlong meeting is spent piecing together what happened and then plotting out a fix. By the time Elman and the CEO turn their attention to the real problem—lack of growth—they're slumped in their chairs. Each exhales deeply and starts spit-balling ideas for turning things around.

"You think going into it, the big hits are where you're going to devote most of your attention, but something like the opposite is true," Elman said after the meeting. The successes largely take care of themselves. It's the start-ups that showed so much promise when he was investing millions, if not tens of millions, of dollars but are now limping along that eat up much of his time and energy. "Things were really going great in the beginning," Elman said of the company he'd just advised. "But then . . ." He left the sentence unfinished and said instead, "That's also venture capital. Even companies you think have the most promise don't always work out."

5

THE APPRENTICE

There are any number of ways of becoming a venture capitalist that don't require first starting a company that makes everyone rich or arriving with a résumé that includes stints at LinkedIn, Twitter, and Facebook. Mike Moritz, who might be the best VC who ever lived, was a journalist, of all things. Moritz was in his early thirties, a staff writer at *Time* magazine and the author of two books—including *The Little Kingdom*, a well-regarded book about the early days at Apple—when in 1986 he was invited to join Sequoia Capital. Since then, he has been an early investor in Yahoo!, Google, PayPal, YouTube, Zappos, Instacart, and Stripe, the last of which was valued at $9.2 billion in 2017. That's only a small share of the Moritz-backed companies that have IPO'd or been bought by a larger firm.

"The rule for getting into venture is that you demonstrate your business acumen as an executive or by starting a company," said start-up lawyer Scott Dettmer. "But there are almost as many exceptions to that rule as people who get into the venture that way." Allen Morgan had been a partner at one of the Valley's best-known law firms when he was invited to join the Mayfield Fund as a general partner. "It's not that unusual for a lawyer to go into venture capital," Morgan said.

Wall Street has served as a reliable route into venture. Mary Meeker, Bill Gurley, and Kirsten Green are among a long list of Wall Street analysts who have made it big as VCs. Meeker is a more typical Wall Street hire in that she has focused on late-stage growth investments since joining Kleiner Perkins in 2010 after more than twenty years as a well-respected internet analyst at Morgan Stanley. Her late-stage investments have included Facebook, Square, Airbnb, Pinterest, Instacart, Snapchat, Spotify, the peer-to-peer site LendingClub, and the traffic and navigation app Waze. In 2017 *Forbes* ranked Meeker sixth on its annual Midas List.

Bill Gurley is also a regular atop the list. (He ranked just behind Meeker in seventh place in 2017 and topped the list in 2013.) Gurley, who played basketball for the University of

Florida (he also earned an MBA at the University of Texas), worked as a design engineer for Compaq Computer before becoming a stock analyst—first at Credit Suisse, once the hottest investment bank in tech, and then at Deutsche Bank, which was trying to be. In the mid-1990s, he jumped to Hummer Winblad Venture Partners, a high-profile firm that fell short of its media hype; and then eighteen months later, in 1999, he joined Benchmark Capital, another high flier but one that exceeded expectations. A $6.7 million investment in eBay in 1997 that two years later was worth more than $4 billion (a return roughly six hundred times its initial investment) put Benchmark on the map, but it's Gurley who has kept it ranked among venture's top firms. These days Gurley is best known as the VC who, in 2011, led the A round in Uber, when $11 million bought 18 percent of the company—an investment that, on paper at least, is probably worth in the tens of billions of dollars. He led Benchmark's A round funding of Snapchat after Josh Elman's colleagues passed on it, along with early investments in OpenTable (restaurant reservations), Grubhub (food delivery), Zillow (real estate), the Knot (a wedding-planning website), and Stitch Fix (a personal shopping service).

Bill Gurley at least joined an established firm when leaving Wall Street for venture. Kirsten Green became a venture capitalist by creating the position for herself. Green, a stock analyst for Montgomery Securities in the late 1990s and early 2000s, left banking in 2003 to start her own hedge fund. But she quickly decided that she didn't like the work and returned the money to her investors. Her new plan had her learning everything she could about venture capital. Starting with a modest grubstake of $25,000, she started building a name for herself as an angel investor. In 2008 Green was part of a $3 million seed round for a piece of a hot menswear start-up called Bonobos, which Walmart bought in 2017 for $310 million. She created Forerunner Ventures with a $5 million investment in 2010 and invested in both prescription glasses maker Warby Parker and the cosmetics retailer Birchbox. She raised $40 million from institutional investors in 2012 and another $75 million two years after that. In 2016 she closed on a $122 million fund. She took on a partner and hired several other people to help her with investments—all of them women—until, in 2017, she added an African American man as an "investor" (VC-talk for not a partner) to her growing team. Green made her first Midas List in 2017 for investments in what the editors of *Forbes* dubbed "two of the biggest e-commerce exits in recent memory": Dollar Shave Club and Jet.com, a fast-growing e-commerce site that Walmart acquired for $3.3 billion that same year.

AND THEN THERE ARE those who have come to venture through what Tod Francis and others call the "apprentice route." These are people who start with a firm after only a year or two in the work world, if not fresh from business school, and learn by watching and doing. The theory is that a firm makes fifteen or twenty or twenty-five investments each year, and patterns emerge, at least to those able to make sense of it all. "The idea is that you get people who are really smart and over time learn from pattern recognition," Tod Francis explained. "The idea is that you do this long enough, you learn the trade by seeing the process happening over and over again."

Francis is blunt about the downside of the apprentice route. For starters, it has fallen out of favor inside many of the top firms. "Look at venture websites," he said. "They're always stressing all their operating experience because that's what entrepreneurs want." Greylock is a case in point.

The old Greylock was based in Boston, and practically all its employees joined the firm after graduating from Harvard Business School. Today Greylock has eleven partners, each of whom logged many years in the work world before coming aboard. Some were founders, while others are, like Elman, in possession of a résumé thick with brand-name hits. "Our bet is that people who have been in these operating roles, that have lived it day in and day out, they are going to go, 'I can see why this could be great,'" managing partner David Sze told *Newsweek* in 2014.

Another drawback is that the apprentice route puts the young VC at a competitive disadvantage with entrepreneurs. According to Francis, "On those deals where an entrepreneur can have his choice of VCs, the question is why you over the other five people they're gonna meet with that day." Eventually the apprentice VC might rack up a few successes and have those to talk about. But until then, "Your argument is that you have all this experience working with companies at this stage, and here's what to expect, and here's what you've seen work in the past, and here's where you've seen companies get into trouble.

"Here's where those who go the 'ops route' have a big advantage," Francis continued. "An entrepreneur can go online and see the background of every person at every firm." He mentioned another Josh at Greylock: Josh McFarland, who had recently been named a partner there. "He worked at Google, he worked at Twitter, he had his own start-up. His street cred is immediate." By contrast, Francis noted, there are those he calls the "school-version VC"—those on an apprentice track. "There are literally entrepreneurs out there who don't want to even talk to the school-version VC because they're like, 'What do they have to offer?'"

Some take the apprentice approach because they can't help themselves—people such as Geoff Yang, a venture star of the 1990s and 2000s whose hits include Excite, Netflix, and TiVo, a digital video recorder. "I've known I've wanted to be a venture capitalist since I was a teenager," Yang said. His mother was an IBM programmer who left the pioneering company briefly to work on a start-up; his father was a chemical engineer. Yang was around fifteen years old when a friend of his parents, a VC who had funded Atari, brought him to his office. Just like that, he was hooked. "I thought it was so cool, getting involved in the business side of making technology happen," Yang recalled. He double majored in electrical engineering and economics at Princeton University because he thought that would be the perfect background for a VC-in-training. He went to work at IBM after graduating—not as a computer programmer, as expected, but in sales and marketing because he thought that experience would make him more marketable to a VC firm.

"I'm always telling kids I talk with that I 'locked and loaded' way too early," Yang reflected. "I tell them, 'You shouldn't commit too early to any one career path.' But then they'll ask me how I got into the venture business." He arrived at IBM just as the company was releasing its groundbreaking PC and loved his time there, but he stayed only two years because his plan said it was time to attend business school. "I was on this road map, which I stayed on for a long while," he said. He got into both Harvard and Stanford, and again his determination to become a VC dictated his decision. "I basically chose Stanford to be near Silicon Valley," he said.

Similarly, he said no to a job offer from the investment bank Goldman Sachs, where he had worked during the summer between his first and second years of business school. "I had this guy come over to my house, the partner in charge of West Coast tech for the firm, yelling at me, 'You're crazy! You're crazy!'" Yang said. "But I told him I'd wanted to be in the venture business forever and wanted at least to try it."

There was no job for him in any of the sun-washed offices along Sand Hill Road, so Yang returned to New York for a job with Smith Barney and First Century Partners, a new entity the investment house had created to enter the venture business. He resented that others in the firm, but not he, were enjoying a share of the profits. He resented, too, intrusions on his time. "I wanted to be a VC," he said. "But they saw me as a resource anyone in the bank could use because I used to work at IBM and knew programming." Even geography seemed to conspire against him. There wasn't much of a tech start-up scene in New York in the mid-1980s when Yang was starting out, so he spent much of each workweek up in the Boston area in search of young companies looking for investors.

When a recruiter called Yang about working as an associate for a new firm called Institutional Venture Partners, or IVP, he jumped at the offer. The situation was similar to the one he'd just left, although this time he was working for a giant of the insurance world, the Fireman's Fund Insurance Company, rather than a bank, which was setting aside a lot of money to enter the venture game. Significantly, though, the new position entailed a return to the West Coast and an opportunity to work with Reid Dennis, an early star of the venture world. In 1987, at age twenty-eight, Yang moved back to the Bay Area. By thirty, he was a full partner in IVP, enjoying his cut of the carry.

Yang was nothing if not rigorous in his approach to venture. He'd work his way through a long list of trade publications, cutting out the product announcements that interested him and then taping them into legal pads organized by sector (PC, networking, peripherals). He attended conferences and emailed academics—who were surprised that anyone outside their small universe even knew there was something called electronic mail. He'd cold-call companies he read about in the trades. "It was a lot less competitive back then," Yang said. "I would call people, and they'd be happy to meet."

VCs tended to be generalists when Yang started. A moneymaking idea was a moneymaking idea. But Yang chose to specialize. "I didn't know how I was going to compete with someone who had a lot more experience, so I picked a couple of industries and focused on those," he said. "I decided my expertise would be the currency on which I traded." Reading through the trades and attending nerd conferences, he learned about the emerging Wide World Web. Yang decided to focus on companies that would foster an interconnected world. He invested in a data management company called SynOptics Communications and then another called Wellfleet. The two merged and became Bay Networks, which the telecommunications company Nortel eventually bought for $7.7 billion. Because of Yang, IVP was also an early investor in Juniper Networks, one of the more successful venture investments of all time. This company, which manufactured the routers and switches and other hardware products that allowed computers to connect, was worth $4.9 billion when it went public four years later—$2 billion more than Netscape. Yang also invested in Foundry Networks, a networking company worth $9 billion on its first day of trading in 1999.

Yang was, in VC-talk, an "infrastructure guy." But he'd become best known in the second half of the 1990s for his investment in Excite. "The plan we came up with after Netscape was to write a series of little checks to a bunch of these smaller companies to see what, if anything, turned up," he said. That's how he came to write a check for

$75,000 to a group of Stanford students behind Excite. IVP followed up with another $1.5 million investment in this internet company, which went public only two years after it was founded. "I didn't mean to," Yang said, "but I ended up on the consumer side of the business." He invested in TiVo when it was still a two-person operation (the company was worth $16 billion after its 1999 IPO) and also in Netflix, a company with an $89 billion market cap at the start of 2018. He had his doubts about a mail-based movie-rental subscription service, but its founder, Reed Hastings, had impressed him. "A lot of the time as a venture capitalist, you're investing in the person or the team rather than the idea," Yang said. He was also an investor in MySpace and Ask Jeeves.

Yang has been hearing the arguments against the apprentice route since he was twenty-six years old and just starting out. But three decades in the business have taught him the downside of the ops route. "Sometimes it's really hard for operations people to realize they don't run anything anymore," he said. He saw this attitude all the time, he said: the former executive from a top tech company who acted as if he were the de facto CEO whenever any big decisions needed to be made. "They'd try to use their board seat to act like an operator, but they had it all wrong," Yang said. "As a board member, my job is to hire and fire the CEO. I can encourage the CEO to my point of view, but if I can't, my job is to encourage and support the CEO."

He might also point to his own track record, and those of people such as Jim Breyer of Facebook fame (whom Accel partners hired straight from Harvard Business School), when making the case for learning the business by doing it rather than first working somewhere else. "When people ask me about breaking into venture," Yang said, "I always tell them, 'If you're ambivalent, go into operations. Learn while you're figuring things out. Go do great things.' But those who are certain they want to be a VC? Why not? Go the apprentice route."

THESE DAYS THERE ARE a lot more Josh Elmans being brought on as partners, especially in early-stage funds, but still plenty of Geoff Yangs and Jim Breyers. Accel hired Peter Fenton after he had earned his MBA at Stanford in 2000. Six years later, he joined Benchmark as a general partner, where he led a $10 million C round in Yelp and backed a twenty-five-employee company called Twitter. Yelp was worth $1.5 billion when it went public in 2012; Twitter, $25 billion at the end of its first day of trading in 2013. On one very good day in 2014, Fenton was able to watch two of his investments go public: data software maker Hortonworks and New Relic, a software analytics company. That same year, another of his companies, Zendesk, a cloud-based customer support start-up, also IPO'd. Fenton ranked third on the 2017 *Forbes* Midas List.

Jeremy Levine is another Midas regular best known for an A round investment in Pinterest. Levine, who has ranked as high as tenth on the Midas List, has a computer science degree from Duke University but no MBA. He worked two years at McKinsey & Company, the giant consulting firm, and two more for a large private equity firm called AEA Investors. His operating experience amounted to two years as the vice president of operations for a small software publisher called Dash before he was hired by Bessemer Venture Partners in New York in 2000. By 2005, he was leading Bessemer's first-round investment in Yelp when the consumer review site was a San Francisco–only site with a hundred thousand users—two years ahead of Peter Fenton. He led a $12.8 million C round in LinkedIn in 2007 and that same year was an early investor in the New Jersey–based Diapers

.com, which Amazon bought three years later for $540 million. In 2010 Levine navigated a $14 million B round in MindBody, which today is a publicly traded $1.4 billion company that sells management software to spas, salons, yoga and dance studios, and personal trainers. And who can say what the $10 million A round he led in Pinterest in 2011 will be worth—except that it will be a lot. The company was valued at more than $12 billion when it raised another $150 million in 2017, suggesting a payoff well in excess of $1 billion.

Nikhil Basu Trivedi from Shasta is another apprentice success story, even if not quite yet as accomplished. Basu Trivedi was thirteen years old and in the eighth grade when his parents, who grew up in India, moved from England to the Bay Area. There his mother taught at the university level, and his father worked at Sun Microsystems, a once-storied Silicon Valley firm with a sprawling campus that now houses Facebook. While attending Menlo, an elite private school just two miles from Sand Hill Road, he met the children of several venture capitalists. "A seed was planted," he said.

At Princeton, he met Taylor Francis, whose father, Tod, is a managing partner at Shasta Ventures. The elder Francis had agreed to judge a business plan competition at his son's school and, in anticipation of the visit, asked his son to invite to dinner the one student he should be sure to meet while he was on campus. Basu Trivedi, several years older than Taylor, didn't know him that well. "I was just like, 'Oh yeah, this kid wants me to meet his dad; we'll have dinner in the dining hall, it'll be great,'" Basu Trivedi said. "I didn't look at as a job- or business-related meeting." Basu Trivedi, who majored in molecular biology at Princeton (with a minor in finance), worked on several start-ups there, including Artsy, which he cofounded during his sophomore year. Today Artsy, which describes itself as a "global platform for discovering and collecting art," employs two hundred people and was valued at $275 million when it raised $50 million in venture financing in 2017.

Yet Basu Trivedi had remained with Artsy only through its seed round of funding. Instead, after graduation, he took a job in New York as an analyst at Insight Venture Partners, a growth-stage venture fund. Meanwhile, Francis made sure that others in the firm met Basu Trivedi. "Whenever someone from Shasta was coming to New York," Basu Trivedi said, "Tod would send me a note and say, 'Hey, I really want you to meet my partner Sean. I want you to meet my partner Jason.' And that's how I got to know the Shasta team." A year after he started at Insight Ventures, in 2012, the Shasta partners invited him to the West Coast to spend the day with them. Not long after he returned to New York, Francis phoned to offer him a job. "I remember Tod saying to me, 'There's no expiration date on this job offer: you can join us next week, you could join us next month, you could join us next year. We just want you to be the next member of the team,'" Basu Trivedi said. He moved back to the Bay Area a few weeks later to start as an associate at Shasta. He was just twenty-three years old. Three years later, he was promoted to principal, which represented a pay increase but meant he still wasn't a full partner.

My meeting Basu Trivedi was a happy accident. Visiting the Bay Area for a final reporting trip for this book, I had arranged to spend a full day with a VC at another highly touted firm before flying back home. But less than twenty-four hours before we were to meet at her offices, the VC changed her mind and canceled. Per chance, the apologetic email from her PR person arrived while I was visiting with Tod Francis, who had gushed about the twenty-eight-year-old phenom working for his firm. "Thoughtful, reflective, young, but not brash," he said of Basu Trivedi. "A disciplined investor, especially for someone his age." Listening to him describe Nikhil, I felt a pang of sadness that my dance card was full. But with suddenly nothing to do the next day, I reached out to Basu Trivedi, who graciously invited me to meet him at midday at Shasta's San Francisco offices and spend the rest of the afternoon with him.

That morning had been a busy one for Basu Trivedi. He had visited with a Shasta portfolio company early in the day and then was on the phone with another to help its founders think through a problem. He then took up residence in a conference room just behind the reception desk for a second meeting with a consumer internet company he thinks might be worth an investment. When I arrived, he was still in the same room but was now meeting for the first time with a trio there to pitch him on "a consumer marketplace business I'm very excited about." Through the glass, I could see the animated Basu Trivedi engaged in conversation. After they'd taken their leave and I was ushered into the same room, he described the meeting as "most stimulating."

"Even if the day is meeting after meeting after meeting, it's energizing to meet with entrepreneurs who are dreaming the next big thing," he said. "Five years later, that never has gone away for me."

Basu Trivedi greeted me dressed casually in jeans, an untucked open-collared gray shirt, and Docksider shoes. He's a slim, good-looking man with a broad smile and a flop of dark hair. "I'd like you to know I answered precisely two emails last night when I got home," he told me in a refined British accent pleasing to the ear. "One was from my girlfriend, the other was from you." He was my hero for bailing me out last minute, but he apologized for having made me wait in the reception area for fifteen minutes and then several more times over the course of the afternoon worried aloud that he wasn't giving me what I needed, despite my repeated assurances that he was. Unfailingly polite, he seemed exactly the person you'd most likely invite to dinner with your dad if he were visiting campus and wanted to meet the most impressive person you know.

Basu Trivedi was only a principal, but already he was serving on the boards of three companies, including the Farmer's Dog, a subscription dog food business based in Brooklyn, New York, which, according to its website, delivers "fresh meals made with healthy, whole food ingredients in personalized meal plans." "I'm pretty young to be leading investments as a venture capitalist," Basu Trivedi acknowledged. "I feel really lucky to be doing this." It seemed only a

matter of waiting for Shasta to raise a new fund for the firm
to officially make him a partner.

"Of the associates I started off with in 2012, even the
older ones, there's only a handful I can think of who are still
at the same firm five years later," he said.

We talked for a while about his life and how he had come
to be a VC while he picked at a salad he had grabbed from
the kitchen. He also told me about the rest of our day. Several years earlier, Peter Thiel's personal foundation, the
Thiel Foundation, had launched a fund called Breakout
Labs to support early-stage companies (according to the
Breakout Labs website) "as they transition radical scien-
tific discoveries out of the lab and into the market." Basu
Trivedi has staked out the consumer internet as his specialty, but he also likes the idea of taking advantage of his
degree in molecular biology and carving out a side interest
in science-based start-ups. With that in mind, he signed up
for Unboxing 2017, where Breakout Labs was showcasing
sixteen of its portfolio companies, each of which was now
seeking a sizable infusion of cash through an A or B round
of venture funding.

On an Uber ride over to a Potrero Hill venue around

ten minutes from his office, Basu Trivedi warned me about happy ears. "The really difficult part of this business, I've learned," he said, "is that a lot of businesses look good, but your job is to figure out if they're amazing." The rejects are easy to dismiss: "You're not that fired up about the people, or you don't think it's a big enough market, or they just don't have enough traction," he explained. "What's hard is when they actually satisfy a bunch of those dimensions. Then the question is whether they'll be this breakout company that can do hundreds of millions or billions in revenue, attain a market cap in the billions, and can deliver a twenty-times return on our investment. Those are the types of things we're thinking about."

I saw what Basu Trivedi meant, as CEOs took turns pitching their companies to a room of a couple of hundred people. If I had a bag of cash, I might have invested in at least half of the sixteen companies presenting. Wearable health monitors that tattoo to your body. A regenerative bone company. Another that regenerated tissue. A next-generation energy start-up. A company working on cheap food tags that will both improve food safety and help reduce food waste. Each was more amazing than the one before it. Basu Trivedi tapped notes on his phone and gamely read aloud what he had written after each presenter. "Not big enough market," he wrote about one. About another: "Great idea, but defensible?" Some of the CEOs were terrific during their five minutes onstage, while others were less impressive. Of one, the ever-polite Basu Trivedi had written, "Not as good a presentation," when a more accurate description would have been "Lousy presentation."

The afternoon was split into two: eight presentations, followed by an extended networking break, and then the remaining eight. We arrived only a minute or two before the program began, so we took seats along the wall near the back doors. Even this more formal part of the program proved to be a social time for Basu Trivedi, as a steady stream of people stopped by to say hello to him. During the break, I felt as though I were with royalty. We couldn't go five feet without him stopping to talk with someone else: another VC, LPs he knew, and other members of the investing community. "Everyone likes Nikhil when they meet him," Francis had told me. "He's this networking machine, not just because he's extroverted but because he's totally genuine."

That night was going to be a big one for him and his girlfriend, who is now his fiancée. It was Diwali, the Hindu festival of lights, and they were attending a celebratory dinner in San Francisco. Basu Trivedi stayed through the last formal presentation but skipped out before the final planned networking session. "Mind if we walk?" he asked. The apprentice proved game to talk about what he was learning as he studied his partners and their practices. For instance, one had taught him to break the job into five easy pieces:

FIND. (Find great companies to consider.)
DECIDE. (Choose those with the potential to be extraordinary.)
WIN. (Make sure the entrepreneurs pick you.)
HELP. (Be there for your portfolio companies.)
EXIT. (The real win for the venture capitalist.)

"It's just these five things," he said. "The problem with venture is, you've got to do it for a long time to be any good at any of them."

Basu Trivedi knows Josh Elman. Of course he does. He laughed when I mentioned that Elman had brought up Snap as the one that got away no fewer than three times during our time together. His was the laugh of someone who lived in a world where bad decisions involving billions of dollars are not that uncommon. I started listing the firms that had passed on Facebook (including Benchmark) and the half dozen I knew of that had turned down an opportunity to invest in Google. "It's so easy to talk yourself out of anything in this business," he said thoughtfully. "Uber, when it started, was just black cars. How big a market is that? How many people out there are going to pay a premium to get a black car using their phone? The smartphone was still very early in penetration. It comes down to believing in the team and in a market that can expand."

We arrive at Basu Trivedi's home, and I use Lyft (I do all I can to avoid using Uber) to take me back to my car. Before I've even reached the lot where the car is parked, he's already sent me an invitation to connect via LinkedIn. I have a new friend.

A few weeks later, I can't say I'm surprised when, reading StrictlyVC, the free daily email I had signed up for at Basu Trivedi's suggestion, I learn that he's been promoted to partner, along with two others that Shasta had been grooming. I send Basu Trivedi a congratulatory note, and his return note includes a gumdrop-shaped orange happy face—his go-to emoji, I'd learn. He thanks me for my good wishes but then asks how the writing is going and wishes me an "early happy Thanksgiving." The working VC is always laying pipe, making connections, leaving behind good impressions for the opportunity to maybe find the next big company.

6

A YOUNGER PERSON'S GAME

Maybe the most discouraging news to people thinking about becoming a VC is that there's something
perfect about the prototypical VC. He or she tends to be
thin and very fit. I'd estimate that 75 percent of the VCs I've
met in the past two decades have received an MBA from
Harvard or Stanford. A big share of the rest hail from a
short list of elite business schools. I've never seen so many
blue eyes per capita than among venture capitalists, and
their smiles tend to be preternaturally pearly white. As a
group, they're exceedingly smart and usually enjoyable to
be around. If there's a "best and the brightest" in this country, the VCs are certainly among them. They're by defini-
tion the elite: the top 1 percent of the top 1 percent.

Venture is a hard world to break into but also one that
rewards success. People raise a modest fund and make
a few smart picks, which lets them raise more money. A

junior-VC-in-training does the same, and suddenly she is no longer an associate but a senior associate with a chance of making principal, if not partner. The product managers and marketing gurus and growth hackers can make names for themselves at growth-stage tech companies that wow the rest of the world and find themselves being invited out for coffee and a conversation that ends with an invitation to join a firm.

"The encouraging news for anyone who dreams of becoming a venture capitalist is it's a younger person's game," Tod Francis said. "It's Nikhil and the younger partners who are hanging out with people starting their own companies five or six or seven days a week."

These are both good times and bad for women seeking to get into venture. There are more opportunities for women but also a bro culture that is endemic to tech. Before there were Harvey Weinstein and the #MeToo movement, there was Susan Fowler, a programmer whose 2017 Medium post detailing the sexual harassment she had endured while working at Uber ("Reflecting on One Very, Very Strange Year at Uber") led to an investigation and spurred the banishment of Travis Kalanick from his own company. A few months after Fowler's post, the venture community was rocked by revelations about Justin Caldbeck, a rising star. He had led investments for Lightspeed Venture Partners (itself a celebrated newcomer to the venture scene) in TaskRabbit and Stitch Fix (valued at $1.4 billion when it IPO'd at the end of 2017). In 2014 Caldbeck cofounded Binary Capital, which was riding high until June 2017, when a tech news site called The Information quoted a half-dozen women claiming unwanted and inappropriate sexual advances by Caldbeck. He apologized publicly to the women he "made feel uncomfortable" and announced that he was taking a leave of absence. Eventually Caldbeck's leave of absence became permanent, and Binary shut its doors.

That fall, another VC, Shervin Pishevar, became another symbol for the industry's bad behavior. Pishevar, an entrepreneur turned angel investor who cofounded his own venture firm in 2013 called Sherpa Capital, was best known for getting into the B round of Uber and investing in both Warby Parker and Airbnb. Bloomberg ran a story quoting multiple women who accused Pishevar of sexual misconduct. Like Caldbeck, Pishevar went on a temporary leave that turned permanent, though he was anything but apologetic. He announced that he would use his newfound free time to pursue a legal case against those he accused of spreading false allegations about him, although he ended up dropping the lawsuit.

Women still face bias inside the venture world. Sequoia, one of the industry's premier firms, didn't hire its first female investing partner until Jess Lee arrived there at the end of 2016. "It only took 44 years," wrote *Fortune* magazine's Kia Kokalitcheva. The consensus choice for the second best venture firm on the planet, Benchmark, didn't add its first woman partner until 2017, when it poached Sarah Tavel from Greylock, where she had also been *its* first woman partner two years earlier. As of this writing, Greylock has no women partners, which is true as well of Bessemer Ventures and Andreessen Horowitz, two more top venture firms. PitchBook Data, a research firm based in Seattle, found that in 2010 that only 5 percent of the partners at the country's larger venture firms (those that had raised a fund of at least $200 million) were women. Incredibly, that figure *dropped* to 4 percent when PitchBook repeated the study in 2014. A more recent study showed it bumping up to 7 percent.

The pressure for change should be more opportunities for a wider pool of venture candidates. "There's a push in Silicon Valley right now around diversity, particularly gender-based diversity, based a lot on the issues raised with Justin Caldbeck and things that came out after that," said Maha Ibrahim of Canaan. "There aren't a lot of us, but the female general partners are getting together and talking about these issues." Much of their effort is focused on mentoring and supporting the women who join their ranks.

"The unfortunate fact is that most women working in venture capital are associates, and often they're the only female in that firm," Ibrahim said. "A lot of them are saying, 'I don't know if I fit; I don't see myself as being supported here.'" Some aren't waiting for acceptance. Jesse Draper, a great-granddaughter of the founder of the first West Coast venture capital firm, William Henry Draper Jr., started her own $10.4 million seed fund, Halogen Ventures, that invests exclusively in female founders. Aileen Lee, who holds a science degree from MIT and an MBA from Harvard, worked for the Gap and then Kleiner Perkins before starting Cowboy Ventures, a seed fund, in 2012. Cowboy can already claim twelve exits in less than six years, including Dollar Shave Club, and today ranks as one of the Valley's premier funds.

Race is a different story. In all my years of visiting venture firms and attending venture-heavy events in the Bay

Area (and, to a lesser extent, in New York), I've seen maybe one or two African American VCs and about the same number who are Latino. That's starting to change at the associates level, and maybe the newest generation of VCs will offer more than lip service about the need for change.

The state of the industry offers more positives for those wanting to enter the venture world. The venture ecosystem is thriving these days. Fund-raising in 2016 was at a healthy $42 billion—the highest figure in ten years. As of 2016, according to the National Venture Capital Association, there were 898 venture firms across the United States. That represents a drop-off of several hundred from the peak days of the late 1990s and the start of the 2000s, but that's probably a positive sign. Venture funds are once again posting double-digit returns. Those in the top quartile are again delivering annualized returns of 25 percent or more. Fewer companies are going public than in the past, but more are being snapped up in mergers and acquisitions.

The rise of the super angel and the blooming of so many seed funds probably represent the two most encouraging trends for wannabe VCs. In the old days, angel investing meant no jobs above that of a personal assistant. No longer. Clicking on the "Meet the Team" tab at websites some of the better-known firms demonstrates that the apprentice route is alive and well, at least at the seed level. Youth seems prized more than experience at firms seeking to fund promising companies that are still being run out of a dorm room; each is populated by people in their twenties and early thirties with profiles that emanate a high-energy, bubbly optimism.

One of the best of this new crop of seed firms is one of the earliest, First Round, founded in 2004 by serial entrepreneur Josh Kopelman. I counted seven partners working for First Round, along with another twenty-nine employees, including a chief financial officer, an office manager, a pitch doctor, several engineers, and Rei Wang, who took over as director of its Dorm Room Fund six years after she graduated from Emory University with a BA in international relations.

That's another route into venture: a role other than that of an investing partner. Greylock has a four-person public relations team headed by the firm's "marketing partner," Elisa Schreiber, who went to work at Greylock three years after earning her MBA at the University of Southern California's business school in 2011. Eight people at the firm work in recruiting. One is Dan Portillo, who turned forty years old in 2017. His father was an undocumented immigrant from El Salvador; his mother, born in Cuba. Portillo was the first in his family to go to college but left the University of California, Los Angeles (UCLA), before graduating to start working as a recruiter for a series of venture-backed start-ups. He would become a "talent partner" at Greylock (he is one of two) in 2013, two years after he started at the firm.

"I look to give any advantage I can to my partners in a competitive situation," Portillo explained. "If they're excited about a potential investment, I'll drop everything to talk talent strategy, to help that start-up recruit." He isn't making investment decisions, which, of course, is central to what a VC does, but there's still the excitement of working with a lot of smart people doing interesting things.

"For those trying to get in, the industry is ripe with opportunity right now," said Ben Veghte, a vice president at the National Venture Capital Association. That's especially true, he added, at the larger firms such as Greylock that are raising billion-dollar funds. "These big firms have employee head counts of a hundred or more. At the same time, we're seeing the emergence of a lot of new players that we would call 'emerging managers,' who are growing and hiring as they raise funds in the range of fifty million to one hundred million. As far as employment opportunities for young graduates and people out there who want to sink their teeth into venture, I think this is a great time to get into the industry."

EPILOGUE

At the start of 2018, Josh Elman began talking to his partners about how they thought he was doing as a VC. "The question I was wrestling with was if I was going to be as successful finding companies worth billions and billions and billions of dollars as I thought I'd be when I was first getting started as a VC," he said. The forty-two-year-old was pleased that his partners thought he was doing well, but those discussions revealed an unhappiness beyond any insecurity he was feeling about his performance.

Elman wasn't enjoying the job as much as he'd thought he would. He brought up his investment in Otto, the digital lock maker that went out of business near the end of 2017. "That whole experience left a bitter taste in my mouth," he said. A larger company had proposed buying Otto for $200 million, but, he said, Otto had rejected the deal. "So instead of showing a modest return on our investment, we're having to shut the business down and lay off sixty people just before Christmas. A couple of experiences like that got me thinking, 'Do I really have what it takes to do this for the next ten years?'"

He took an inventory of the things he didn't like about being a VC. The solo nature of the job wasn't for him, and he worried constantly that a single stray comment or moment would mean not landing that next billion-dollar deal because he had been in a bad mood when someone approached him on the street with his kids or he was caught glancing at his phone during a pitch. He didn't like being drawn into a dozen different directions at once and confessed to those around him that he wasn't doing as well as he made out. It didn't help Elman's psyche that he felt so strongly the let down of the companies that didn't work out. There was also the lure of the start-up world. Not for the first time, he spoke about the disappointment he felt having never really experienced what he called "the full rocket ride." He had left LinkedIn just as it was taking off and fled Facebook even though he knew it was about to go global. And then there was the disappointment of being pushed out of Twitter a couple of years before its IPO.

"Talking with my partners, they were 'Hey, man, this might not be where you're going to excel the most. What you do really well is build stuff, so maybe you need to be building stuff rather than helping others do it.'" Conversations with friends and mentors, he said, "made me realize my happiest times are when I'm deep into a project, working with a group of people trying to build something really great." His task would be to find a company with the potential to "shoot the moon"—as when in the card game Hearts you end up with all the cards that matter.

Elman didn't leave Greylock altogether. He's still a "venture partner" with the firm. That's an elastic phrase that can mean whatever its users want it to mean, but, in Elman's case, he'll continue tending to the companies that he brought to Greylock as well as "source" future deals—meaning that he'll point promising deals its way if he hears about something. Beyond that, there was a vague promise to help the firm "on future deals that are in my areas of expertise."

It didn't take Elman long to hit upon his next venture. Finding a hot tech company with boundless potential can be like hailing a car in today's environment, especially living and working around Sand Hill Road. Wave your arm or tap a few times on a screen, and there's bound to be one around the corner. In mid-March—roughly eight weeks after first broaching the topic with his partners—Greylock announced that Elman was joining Robinhood, an app that lets customers buy and sell stock without a commission. Elman would be vice president of product for this Palo Alto–based company with 170 employees when he joined and a valuation of around $5 billion. By that point, Robinhood had already attained roughly the same number of customers—three million—as E-Trade Financial Corporation, the big discount broker. Apparently, Elman sees the potential for a lot more growth. "The best experience for me in my life has been working my ass off for a single company and bringing it to millions and millions of people," he said.

Greylock's David Sze said he wasn't surprised by the news. "If we believe that operators make the best investors, then we have to accept that a few of us will want to go back to being operators," he observed. Sze offered the example of another recent departure, Joseph Ansanelli, who, like Elman, had been a general partner for the firm until he wasn't. Ansanelli, a well-known serial entrepreneur in Silicon Valley, had joined Greylock as a partner in 2012. (A company he'd cofounded, Vontu, was sold to Symantec for $350 million; another of his companies went public; and a third was bought by Apple.) Yet by the start of 2018, Ansanelli had cofounded yet another company, called Gladly. He, too, was now a "venture partner" at the firm.

"VC is a tough gig," Sze said. "There's constant pressure to earn returns. The grind and hustle can be very hard." He wished his friend Josh well ("I am glad he found clarity on what makes him happy"), but he also had a firm to run. He and his partners had $1 billion or more to invest, and, with Elman's and Ansanelli's departures, they were now down two VCs. That was good news for the Valley's junior VCs, many of whom (though hardly all of them) were looking to continue in a profession that fewer people seem to truly enjoy than one might think, given the compensation and the rush and the sense among many that to become a VC is to have ascended to the top of a very high mountain.

ACKNOWLEDGMENTS

First, thanks to Jonathan Karp, president and publisher of Simon & Schuster, and Ben Loehnen, my editor there, for asking if I'd be interested in writing a few books for a proposed series about "becoming." It seemed the latest great idea from the fertile mind of the incomparable Jon Karp and another chance to work with the talented Ben, who had so ably served as my counsel and editor on *Katrina: After the Flood*, my latest book and, not incidentally, I think, my best.

Not thirty minutes after receiving an email invitation from Ben, I had written back, "First impression: I love this idea. And if it works out, I'm claiming venture capital." Venture capital is an all-time favorite topic of mine. I relished a chance to spend time with and write about these high-stakes gamblers and risk takers.

As always, I'm grateful for the World's Greatest Agent, Elizabeth Kaplan, who has always been in my corner. I appreciate the great care that Phil Bashe took while copyediting my manuscript, and thanks, too, to Amar Deol at Simon & Schuster, who was always there to aid and assist in the name of a manuscript. And thanks also to Rachel Caspert, a master at Excel and a favorite numbers cruncher.

A big shout-out to Elisa Schreiber at Greylock, who was a dream to work with, and also David Sze, the firm's managing partner and industry mensch. They opened the door for me at Greylock, pointed the way to Josh Elman, and then let me do my job. Big thanks as well to Tod Francis, who bailed me out with an introduction to the impressive Nikhil Basu Trivedi, who was a delight to spend time with.

It had been some years since I had covered Silicon Valley. I was pleased that, in my absence, sites such as VentureBeat had popped up to keep closer tabs on venture. While working on this book, I grew to appreciate the job *Forbes* does each year with its Midas List, which offers a fun glimpse into the venture world; to wit, a terrific piece by George Anders with Alex Konrad, "Inside Sequoia Capital: Silicon Valley's Innovation Factory," that the magazine ran to accompany its 2014 list. While researching this book I also developed a deep dependency on Crunchbase, the database of venture deals the website TechCrunch maintains.

TechCrunch was a mere infant when I left the tech beat in 2005 (the journalist's peripatetic life: reassigned to the Gulf Coast to write about New Orleans's recovery post-Katrina) but has grown into an impressive adult, cheeky and informed and smart. Also of note: Recode, which has also grown into a full-blown news outfit in my absence, and Connie Loizos, Silicon Valley editor of TechCrunch and author of StrictlyVC, a daily email that kept me entertained and up to date. I also became a fan of The Information, which for my money (if I could afford an annual subscription; thanks again, Miguel!), is the best source for what's really happening in Silicon Valley and tech.

Last but hardly least, my family. With gratitude and love to Daisy Walker, who is always my first best editor (and also my spouse), and our two boys, Oliver and Silas, who keep a smile on my face (if not also occasionally causing a growly sound to emit from my mouth). With love.

FURTHER READING

There haven't been many books written about venture capital. I've come across only one great journalistic account that brings the reader inside a venture firm: *eBoys* by Randall E. Stross, published in 2000. Stross chose wisely when zeroing on Benchmark, then a newly minted firm with a lot of buzz but no track record. A historian by training, Stross describes himself as a "writer-in-residence" inside Benchmark from 1997 to 1999. The resulting book gives a great sense of time and place while introducing readers to the six tall men (their average height is six feet, five inches) who backed eBay, Webvan, and other billion-dollar start-ups. Stross was there when eBay was a small thirty-person start-up eager for attention and there after its 1998 IPO—much to the chagrin of at least some of the partners, embarrassed by the unimaginable wealth they were pocketing. On his watch, each of the six partners had increased his net worth by approximately $350 million. Benchmark has been press shy ever since.

If you are looking to better understand the nitty-gritty of venture finance, there's no better book than *Venture Deals* by Brad Feld, one of the venture world's more well-respected practitioners, and Jason Mendelson, one of his partners. The book offers a readable primer on everything from the basics of a venture term sheet to negotiating tactics to the specific issues likely to come up at every round of funding. I'll quote Dick Costello, the former CEO of Twitter, who said in an endorsement of the book that he wished this book had been around in his time to save him from having to learn "all the tricks, traps, and nuances on my own."

ABOUT THE AUTHOR

GARY RIVLIN is a Pulitzer Prize–winning investigative reporter and the author of five books, including *Katrina: After the Flood*. His work has appeared in *The New York Times Magazine*, *Mother Jones*, *GQ*, and *Wired*, among other publications. He is a two-time Gerald Loeb Award winner and former reporter for the *New York Times*. He lives in New York with his wife, theater director Daisy Walker, and two sons.